THE NATURE PHILOSOPHY

ARVIND UPADHYAY

In this hilltop orchard overlooking the Inland Sea stand several mud-walled huts. Here, young people from the cities—some from other lands—live a crude, simple life growing crops. They live self-sufficiently on a diet of brown rice and vegetables, without electricity or running water. These young fugitives, disaffected with the cities or religion, tread through my fields clad only in a loincloth. The search for the bluebird of happiness brings them to my farm in one corner of Iyo-shi in Ehime Prefecture, where they learn how to become quarter-acre farmers. Chickens run free through the orchard and semi-wild vegetables grow in the clover among the trees. In the paddy fields spread out below on the Dogo Plain, one no longer sees the pastoral green of barley and the blossoms of rape and clover from another age. Instead, desolate fields lie fallow, the crumbling bundles of straw portraying the chaos of modern farming practices and the confusion in the hearts of farmers. Only my field lies covered in the fresh green of winter grain. (*Barley or wheat. Barley cultivation is predominant in Japan, but most of what I say about barley in this book applies equally well to wheat.) This field has not been plowed or turned in over thirty years. Nor have I applied chemical fertilizers or prepared compost, or sprayed pesticides or other chemicals. I practice what I call "do-nothing" farming here, yet each year I harvest close to 22 bushels (1,300 pounds) of winter grain and 22 bushels of rice per quarter-acre. My goal is to eventually take in 33 bushels per quarter-acre. Growing grain in this way is very easy and straightforward. I simply broadcast clover and winter grain over the ripening heads of rice before the fall harvest. Later, I harvest the rice while treading on the young shoots of winter grain. After leaving the rice to dry for three days, I thresh it then scatter the straw uncut over the entire field. If I have some chicken droppings on hand, I scatter this over the straw. Next, I form clay pellets containing seed rice and scatter the pellets over the straw before the New Year. With the winter grain growing and the rice seed sown, there is now nothing left to do until the harvesting of the winter grain. The labor of one or two people is more than enough to grow crops on a quarter-acre. In late May, while harvesting the winter grain, I notice the clover growing luxuriantly at my feet and the small shoots that have emerged from the rice seed in the clay pellets. After harvesting, drying, and threshing the winter grain, I scatter all of the straw uncut over the field. I then flood the field for four to five days to weaken the clover and give the rice shoots a chance to break through the cover of clover. In June and July, I leave the field unirrigated, and in August I run water through the drainage ditches* once every week or ten days. That is essentially all there is to the method of natural farming I call "direct-seeded, no-tillage, winter grain/rice succession in a clover cover." Were I to say that all my method of farming boils down to is the symbiosis of rice and barley or wheat in clover, I would probably be reproached: "If that's all there is to growing rice, then farmers wouldn't be out there working so hard in their fields." Yet, that is all there is to it. Indeed, with this method I have consistently gotten better-thanaverage yields. Such being the case, the only conclusion possible is that there must be something drastically wrong with farming practices that require so much unnecessary labor. Scientists are always saying, "Let's try this, let's try that." Agriculture becomes swept up in all of this fiddling around; new methods requiring additional expenditures and effort by farmers are constantly introduced, along with new pesticides and fertilizers. As for me, I have taken the opposite tack. I eliminate unnecessary practices, expenditures, and labor by telling myself, "I don't need to do this, I don't need to do that." After thirty years at it, I have managed to reduce my labor to essentially just sowing seed and spreading straw. Human effort is unnecessary because nature, not man, grows the rice and wheat. If you stop and think about it, every time someone says "this is useful," "that has value," or "one ought to do such-and-such," it is because man has created the preconditions that give this whatever-it-is its value. We create situations in which, without something we never needed in the first place, we are lost. And to get ourselves out of such a predicament, we make what appear to be new discoveries, which we then herald as progress. Flood a field with water, stir it up with a plow and the ground will set as hard as plaster. If the soil dies and hardens, then it must be plowed each year to soften it. All we are doing is creating the conditions that make a plow useful, then rejoicing at the utility of our tool. No plant on the face of the earth is so weak as to germinate only in plowed soil. Man has no need to plow and turn the earth, for microorganisms and small animals act as nature's tillers. By killing the soil with plow and chemical fertilizer, and rotting the roots through prolonged summer flooding, farmers create weak, diseased rice plants that require the nutritive boost of chemical fertilizers and the protection of pesticides. Healthy rice plants have no need for the plow or chemicals. And compost does not have to be prepared if rice straw is applied to the fields half a year before the rice is sown. Soil enriches itself year in and year out without man having to lift a finger. On the other hand, pesticides ruin the soil and create a pollution problem. Shrines in Japanese villages are often surrounded by a grove of tall trees. These trees were not grown with the aid of nutrition science, nor were they protected by plant ecology. Saved from the axe and saw by the shrine deity, they grew into large trees of their own accord. Properly speaking, nature is neither living nor dead. Nor is it small or large, weak or strong, feeble or thriving. It is those who believe only in science who call an insect either a pest or a predator and cry out that nature is a violent world of relativity and contradiction in which the strong feed on the weak. Notions of right and wrong, good and bad, are alien to nature. These are only distinctions invented by man. Nature maintained a great harmony without such notions, and brought forth the grasses and trees without the "helping" hand of man. The living and holistic biosystem that is nature cannot be dissected or resolved into its parts. Once broken down, it dies. Or rather, those who break off a piece of nature lay hold of something that is dead, and, unaware that what they are examining is no longer what they think it to be, claim to understand nature. Man commits a grave error when he collects data and findings piecemeal on a dead and fragmented nature and claims to "know," "use," or "conquer" nature. Because he starts off with misconceptions about nature and takes the wrong approach to understanding it, regardless of how rational his thinking, everything winds up all wrong. We must become aware of the insignificance of human knowledge and activity, and begin by grasping their uselessness and futility. Follow the Workings of Nature We often speak of "producing food," but farmers do not produce the food of life. Only nature has the power to produce something from nothing. Farmers merely assist nature. Modern agriculture is just another processing industry that uses oil energy in the form of fertilizers, pesticides, and machinery to manufacture synthetic food products which are poor imitations of natural food. The farmer today has become a hired hand of industrialized society. He tries without success to make money at farming with synthetic chemicals, a feat that would tax even the powers of the Thousand-Handed Goddess of Mercy. It is no surprise then that he is spinning around like a top. Natural farming, the true and original form of agriculture, is the methodless method of nature, the unmoving way of Bodhidharma. Although appearing fragile and vulnerable, it is potent for it brings victory unfought; it is a Buddhist way of farming that is boundless and yielding, and leaves the soil, the plants, and the insects to themselves.As I walk through the paddy field, spiders and frogs scramble about, locusts jump up, and droves of dragonflies hover overhead. Whenever a large outbreak of leafhoppers occurs, the spiders multiply too, *without fail. Although the yield of this field varies from year to year, there are generally about 250 heads of grain per square yard. With an average of 200 grains per head, this gives a harvest of some 33 bushels for every quarteracre.*

Those who see the sturdy heads of rice rising from the field marvel at the strength and vigor of the plants and their large yields. No matter that there are insect pests here. As long as their natural enemies are also present, a natural balance asserts itself. Because it is founded upon principles derived from a fundamental view of nature, natural farming remains current and applicable in any age. Although ancient, it is also forever new. Of course, such a way of natural farming must be able to weather the criticism of science. The question of greatest concern is whether this "green philosophy" and way of farming has the power to criticize science and guide man onto the road back to nature. The Illusions of Modern Scientific Farming With the growing popularity of natural foods lately, 1 thought that natural farming too would be studied at last by scientists and receives the attention it is due. Alas, I was wrong. Although some research is being conducted on natural farming, most of it remains strictly within the scope of scientific agriculture as practiced to date. This research adopts the basic framework of natural farming, but makes not the slightest reduction in the use of chemical fertilizers and pesticides; even the equipment used has gotten larger and larger. Why do things turn out this way? Because scientists believe that, by adding technical know-how to natural farming, which already reaps over 22 bushels of rice per quarter acre, they will develop an even better method of cultivation and higher yields. Although such reasoning appears to make sense, one cannot ignore the basic contradiction it entails. Until the day that people understand what is meant by "doing nothing"—the ultimate goal of natural farming, they will not relinquish their faith in the omnipotence of science. When we compare natural farming and scientific farming graphically, we can right away appreciate the differences between the two methods. The objective of natural farming is non-action and a return to nature; it is centrifugal and convergent. On the other hand, scientific farming breaks away from nature with the expansion of human wants and desires; it is centripetal and divergent. Because this outward expansion cannot be stopped, scientific farming is doomed to extinction. The addition of new technology only makes it more complex and diversified, generating everincreasing expense and labor. In contrast, not only is natural farming simple, it is also economical and labor-saving. Why is it that, even when the advantages are so clear and irrefutable, man is unable to walk away from scientific agriculture? People think, no doubt, that "doing nothing" is defeatist, that it hurts production and productivity. Yet, does natural farming harm productivity? Far from it. In fact, if we base our figures on the efficiency of energy used in production, natural farming turns out to be the most productive method of farming there is. Natural farming produces 130 pounds of rice—or 200,000 kilocalories of energy —per man-day of labor, without the input of any outside materials. This is about 100 times the daily intake of 2,000 kilocalories by a farmer on a natural diet. Ten times as much energy was expended in traditional farming, which used horses and oxen to plow the fields. The energy input in calories was doubled again with the advent of small-scale mechanization, and doubled yet another time with the shift to large-scale mechanization. This geometric progression has given us the energy-intensive agricultural methods of today. The claim is often made that mechanization has increased the efficiency of work, but farmers must use the extra hours away from their fields to earn outside income to help pay for their equipment. All they have done is exchange their work in the fields for a job in some company; they have traded the joy of working outdoors in the open fields for dreary hours of labor shut up inside a factory. People believe that modern agriculture can both improve productivity and increase yields. What a misconception. The truth of the matter is that the yields provided by scientific farming are smaller than the yields attainable under the full powers of nature.

High-yield practices and scientific methods of increasing production are thought to have given us increased yields that exceed the natural productivity of the land, but this is not so. These are merely endeavors by man to artificially restore full productivity after he has hamstrung nature so that it cannot exercise its full powers. Man creates adverse conditions, then rejoices later at his "conquest" of nature. High-yield technologies are no more than glorified attempts to stave off reductions in productivity. Nor is science a match for nature in terms of the quality of the food it helps to create. Ever since man deluded himself into thinking that nature can be understood by being broken down and analyzed, scientific farming has produced artificial, deformed food. Modern agriculture has created nothing from nature. Rather, by making quantitative and qualitative changes in certain aspects of nature, it has managed only to fabricate synthetic food products that are crude, expensive, and further alienate man from nature. Humanity has left the bosom of nature and recently begun to view with growing alarm its plight as orphan of the universe. Yet, even when he tries returning to nature, man finds that he no longer knows what nature is, and that, moreover, he has destroyed and forever lost the nature he seeks to return to. Scientists envision domed cities of the future in which enormous heaters, air conditioners, and ventilators will provide comfortable living conditions throughout the year. They dream of building underground cities and colonies on the seafloor. But the city dweller is dying; he has forgotten the bright rays of the sun, the green fields, the plants and animals, and the sensation of a gentle breeze on the skin. Man can live a true life only with nature. Natural farming is a Buddhist way of farming that originates in the philosophy of "Mu," or nothingness, and returns to a "do-nothing" nature. The young people living in my orchard carry with them the hope of someday resolving the great problems of our world that cannot be solved by science and reason. Mere dreams perhaps, but these hold the key to the future.

Contents

Preface

Natural farming is based on a nature free of human meddling and intervention. It strives to restore nature from the destruction wrought by human knowledge and action, and to resurrect a humanity divorced from God. While still a youth, a certain turn of events set me out on the proud and lonely road back to nature. With sadness, though, I learned that one person cannot live alone. One either lives in association with people or in communion with nature. I found also, to my despair, that people were no longer truly human, and nature no longer truly natural. The noble road that rises above the world of relativity was too steep for me. These writings are the record of one farmer who for fifty years has wandered about in search of nature. I have traveled a long way, yet as night falls there remains still a long way to go. Of course, in a sense, natural farming will never be perfected. It will not see general application in its true form, and will serve only as a brake to slow the mad onslaught of scientific agriculture. Ever since I began proposing a way of farming in step with nature, I have sought to demonstrate the validity of five major principles: no tillage, no fertilizer, no pesticides, no weeding, and no pruning. During the many years that have elapsed since, I have never once doubted the possibilities of a natural way of farming that renounces alt human knowledge and intervention. To the scientist convinced that nature can be understood and used through the human intellect and action, natural farming is a special case and has no universality. Yet these basic principles apply everywhere. The trees and grasses release seeds that fall to the ground, there to germinate and grow into new plants. The seeds sown by nature are not so weak as to grow only in plowed fields. Plants have always grown by direct seeding, without tillage. The soil in the fields is worked by small animals and roots, and enriched by green manure plants. Only over the last fifty years or so have chemical fertilizers become thought of as indispensable. True, the ancient practice of using manure and compost does help speed crop growth, but this also depletes the land from which the organic material in the compost is taken. Even organic farming, which everyone is making such a big fuss over lately, is just another type of scientific farming. A lot of trouble is taken to move organic materials first Here then there, to process and treat. But any gains to be had from all this activity are local and temporal gains. In fact, when examined from a broader perspective, many such efforts to protect the natural ecology are actually destructive. Although a thousand diseases attack plants in the fields and forests, nature strikes a balance; there never was any need for pesticides. Man grew confused when he identified these diseases as insect damage; he created with his own hands the need for labor and toil. Man tries also to control weeds, but nature does not arbitrarily call one plant a weed and try to eradicate it. Nor does a fruit tree always grow more vigorously and bear more fruit when pruned. A tree grows best in its natural habit; the branches do not tangle, sunlight falls on every leaf, and the tree bears fully each year, not only in alternate years. Many people are worried today over the drying out of arable lands and the loss of vegetation throughout the world, but there is no doubting that human civilization and the misguided methods of crop cultivation that arose from man's arrogance are largely responsible for this global plight. Overgrazing by large animal herds kept by nomadic peoples has reduced the variety of vegetation, denuding the land. Agricultural societies too, with the shift to modern agriculture and its heavy reliance on petroleum-based chemicals, have had to confront the problem of rapid debilitation of the land. Once we accept that nature has been harmed by human knowledge and action, and renounce these instruments of chaos and destruction, nature will recover its ability to nurture all forms of life. In a sense, my path to natural farming is a first step toward the restoration of nature. That natural farming has yet to gain wide acceptance shows just how mortally nature has been afflicted by man's tampering and the extent to which the human spirit has been ravaged and ruined. All of which makes the mission of natural farming that much more critical. I have begun thinking that the natural farming experience may be of some help, however small, in revegetating the world and stabilizing food supply. Although some will call the idea outlandish, I propose that the seeds of certain plants be sown over the deserts in clay pellets to help green these barren lands. These pellets can be prepared by first mixing the seeds of green manure trees —such as black wattle—that grow in areas with an annual rainfall of less than 2 inches, and the seeds of clover, alfalfa, bur clover, and other types of green manure, with grain and vegetable seeds. The mixture of seeds is coated first with a layer of soil, then one of clay, to form microbe-containing clay pellets. These finished pellets could then be scattered by hand over the deserts and savannahs. Once scattered, the seeds within the hard clay pellets will not sprout until rain has fallen and conditions are just right for germination. Nor will they be eaten by mice and birds. A year later, several of the plants will survive, giving a clue as to what is suited to the climate and land. In certain countries to the south, there are reported to be plants that grow on rocks and trees that store water. Anything will do, as long as we get the deserts blanketed rapidly with a green cover of grass. This will bring back the rains. While standing in an American desert, I suddenly realized that rain does not fall from the heavens; it issues forth from the ground. Deserts do not form because there is no rain; rather, rain ceases to fall because the vegetation has disappeared. Building a dam in the desert is an attempt to treat the symptoms of the disease, but is not a strategy for increasing rainfall. First we have to learn how to restore the ancient forests. But we do not have time to launch a scientific study to determine why the deserts are spreading in the first place. Even were we to try, we would find that no matter how far back into the past we go in search of causes, these causes are preceded by other causes in an endless chain of interwoven events and factors that is beyond man's powers of comprehension. Suppose that man were able in this way to learn which plant had been the first to die off in a land turned to desert. He would still not know enough to decide whether to begin by planting the first type of vegetation to disappear or the last to survive. The reason is simple: in nature, there is no cause and effect. Science rarely looks to microorganisms for an understanding of large causal relationships. True, the perishing of vegetation may have triggered a drought, but the plants may have died as a result of the action of some microorganism. However, botanists are not to be bothered with microorganisms as these lie outside their field of interest. We've gathered together such a diverse collection of specialists that we've lost sight of both the starting line and the finish line. That is why I believe that the only effective approach we can take to revegetating barren land is to leave things largely up to nature. One gram of soil on my farm contains about 100 million nitrogen-fixing bacteria and other soil-enriching microbes. I feel that soil containing seeds and these microorganisms could be the spark that restores the deserts. I have created, together with the insects in my fields, a new strain of rice I call "Happy Hill." This is a hardy strain with the blood of wild variants in it, yet it is also one of the highest yielding strains of rice in the world. If a single head of Happy Hill were sent across the sea to a country where food is scarce and there sown over a ten-square-yard area, a single grain would yield 5,000 grains in one year's time. There would be grain enough to sow a half-acre the following year, fifty acres two years hence, and 7,000 acres in the fourth year. This could become the seed rice for an entire nation. This handful of grain could open up the road to independence for a starving people. But the seed rice must be delivered as soon as possible. Even one person can begin. I could be no happier than if my humble experience with natural farming were to be used toward this end. My greatest fear today is that of nature being made the plaything of the human intellect. There is also the danger that man will attempt to protect nature through the medium of human knowledge, without noticing that nature can be restored only by abandoning our preoccupation with knowledge and action that has driven it to the wall. All begins by relinquishing human knowledge. Although perhaps just the empty dream of a farmer who has sought in vain to return to nature and the side of God, I wish to become the sower of seed. Nothing would give me more joy than to meet others of the same mind.

1

Man Cannot Know Nature

Man prides himself on being the only creature on earth with the ability to think. He claims to know himself and the natural world, and believes he can use nature as he pleases. He is convinced, moreover, that intelligence is strength, that anything he desires is within his reach. As he has forged ahead, making new advances in the natural sciences and dizzily expanding his materialistic culture, man has grown estranged from nature and ended by building a civilization all his own, like a wayward child rebelling against its mother. But all his vast cities and frenetic activity have brought him are empty, dehumanized pleasures and the destruction of his living environment through the abusive exploitation of nature. Harsh retribution for straying from nature and plundering its riches has begun to appear in the form of depleted natural resources and food crises, throwing a dark shadow over the future of mankind. Having finally grown aware of the gravity of the situation, man has begun to think seriously about what should be done. But unless he is willing to undertake the most fundamental self-reflection he will be unable to steer away from a path of certain destruction. Alienated from nature, human existence becomes a void, the wellspring of life and spiritual growth gone utterly dry. Man grows ever more ill and weary in the midst of his curious civilization that is but a struggle over a tiny bit of time and space. Leave Nature Alone Man has always deluded himself into thinking that he knows nature and is free to use it as he wishes to build his civilizations. But nature cannot be explained or expanded upon. As an organic whole, it not subject to man's classifications; nor does it tolerate dissection and analysis. Once broken down, nature cannot be returned to its original state. All that remains is an empty skeleton devoid of the true essence of living nature. This skeletal image only serves to confuse man and lead him further astray. Scientific reasoning also is of no avail in helping man understand nature and add to its creations.

Nature as perceived by man through discriminating knowledge is a falsehood. Man can never truly know even a single leaf or a single handful of earth. Unable to fully comprehend plant life and soil, he sees these only through the filter of human intellect. Although he may seek to return to the bosom of nature or use it to his advantage, man only touches one tiny part of nature—a dead portion at that—and has no affinity with the main body of living nature. He is, in effect, merely toying with delusions. Man is but an arrogant fool who vainly believes that he knows all of nature and can achieve anything he sets his mind to. Seeing neither the logic nor order inherent in nature, he has selfishly appropriated it to his own ends and destroyed it. The world today is in such a sad state because man has not felt compelled to reflect upon the dangers of his high-handed ways. The earth is an organically interwoven community of plants, animals, and microorganisms. When seen through man's eyes, it appears either as a model of the strong consuming the weak or of coexistence and mutual benefit. Yet there are food chains and cycles of matter; there is endless transformation without birth or death. Although this flux of matter and the cycles in the biosphere can be perceived only through direct intuition, our unswerving faith in the omnipotence of science has led us to analyze and study these phenomena, raining down destruction upon the world of living things and throwing nature as we see it into disarray. A case in point is the application of toxic pesticides to apple trees and hothouse strawberries. This kills off pollinating insects such as bees and gadflies, forcing man to collect the pollen himself and artificially pollinate each of the blossoms. Although he cannot even hope to replace the myriad activities of all the plants, animals, and microorganisms in nature, man goes out of his way to block their activities, then studies each of these functions carefully and attempts to find substitutes. What a ridiculous waste of effort. Consider the case of the scientist who studies mice and develops a rodenticide. He does so without understanding why mice nourished in the first place. He simply decides that killing them is a good idea without first determining whether the mice multiplied as the result of a breakdown in the balance of nature, or whether they support that balance. The rodenticide is a temporary expedient that answers only the needs of a given time and place; it is not a responsible action in keeping with the true cycles of nature. Man cannot possibly replace all the functions of plants and animals on this earth through scientific analysis and human knowledge. While unable to fully grasp the totality of these interrelationships, any rash endeavor such as the selective extermination or raising of a species only serves to upset the balance and order of nature. Even the replanting of mountain forests may be seen as destructive. Trees are logged for their value as lumber, and species of economic value to man, such as pine and cedar, are planted in large number. We even go so far as to call this "forestry conservation." However, altering the tree cover on a mountain produces changes in the characteristics of the forest soil, which in turn affects the plants and animals that inhabit the forest. Qualitative changes also take place in the air and temperature of the forest, causing subtle changes in weather and affecting the microbial world. No matter how closely one looks, there is no limit to the complexity and detail with which nature interacts to effect constant, organic change. When a section of the forest is clear-cut and cedar trees planted, for example, there no longer is enough food for small birds. These disappear, allowing long-horned beetles to flourish. The beetles are vectors for nematodes, which attack red pines and feed on parasitic Botrytis fungi in the trunks of the pine trees. The pines fall victim to the Botrytis fungi because they are weakened by the disappearance of the edible matsutake fungus that lives symbolically on the roots of red pines. This beneficial fungus has died off as a result of an increase in the harmful Botrytis fungus in the soil, which is itself a consequence of the acidity of the soil. The high soil acidity is the result of atmospheric pollution and acid rain, and so on and so forth. This backward regression from effect to prior cause Continues in an unending chain that leaves one wondering what the true cause is. When the pines die, thickets of bamboo grass rise up. Mice feed on the abundant bamboo grass berries and multiply. The mice attack the cedar saplings, so man applies a rodenticide. But as the mice vanish, a decline occurs in the weasels and snakes that feed on them. To protect the weasels, man then begins to raise mice to restore the roden population. Isn't this the stuff of crazed dreams? Toxic chemicals are applied at least eight times a year on Japanese rice fields. Is it not odd then that hardly any agricultural scientists have bothered to investigate why the amount of insect damage in these fields remains largely the same as in fields where no pesticides are used? The first application of pesticide does not kill off the hordes of rice leafhoppers, but the tens of thousands of young spiders on each square yard of land simply vanish, and the swarms of fireflies that fly up from the stands of grass disappear at once. The second application kills off the chalcid dies, which are important natural predators, and leaves victim dragonfly larvae, tadpoles, and loaches. Just one look at this slaughter would suffice to show the insanity of the blanket application of pesticides. No matter how hard he tries, man can never rule over nature. What he can do is serve nature, which means living in accordance with its laws. The "Do-Nothing" Movement The age of aggressive expansion in our materialistic culture is at an end, and a new "do-nothing" age of consolidation and convergence has arrived. Man must hurry to establish a new way of life and a spiritual culture founded on communion with nature, lest he grow ever more weak and feeble while running around in a frenzy of wasted effort and confusion. When he turns back to nature and seeks to learn the essence of a tree or a blade of grass, man will have no need for human knowledge. It will be enough to live in concert with nature, free of plans, designs, and effort. One can break free of the false image of nature conceived by the human intellect only by becoming detached and earnestly begging for a return to the absolute realm of nature. No, not even entreaty and supplication are necessary; it is enough only to farm the earth free of concern and desire. To achieve a humanity and a society founded on non-action, man must look back over everything he has done and rid himself one by one of the false visions and concepts that permeate him and his society. This is what the "do-nothing" movement is all about. Natural farming can be seen as one branch of this movement. Human knowledge and effort expand and grow increasingly complex and wasteful without limit. We need to halt this expansion, to converge, simplify, and reduce our knowledge and effort. This is in keeping with the laws of nature. Natural farming is more than just a revolution in agricultural techniques. It is the practical foundation of a spiritual movement, of a revolution to change the way man lives.

2

Life in the Farming Villages of the Past

In earlier days, Japanese peasants were a poor and downtrodden lot. Forever oppressed by those in power, they occupied the lowest rung on the social ladder. Where did they find the strength to endure their poverty and what did they depend on to live? The farmers who lived quietly in a secluded inland glen, on a solitary island in the southern seas, or in a desolate northern region of deep snows were self-supporting and independent; they lived a proud, happy, noble life in the great outdoors. People born in remote areas who lived out poor lives and died anonymously were able to subsist in a world cut off from the rest of mankind without discontent or anxiety because, though they appeared alone, they were not. They were creatures of nature, and being close to God (nature incarnate), experienced the daily joy and pride of tending the gardens of God. They went out to work in the fields at sunrise and returned home to rest at sunset, living each day well, one day being as wide and infinite as the universe and yet just one small frame in the unending flow of existence. Theirs was a farming way of life, set in the midst of nature, which violated nothing and was not itself violated. Farmers are bound to take offense when the clever ones who left the village and made their way in the world come back, saying "sir, sir" with false humility, then, when you least expect it, telling you, in effect, to "go to hell." Although farmers have no need for business cards, on occasion they have been misers too mean to part with a single penny, and at other times, millionaires without the slightest interest in fabulous riches. Peasant villages were lonely, out-of-the-way places inhabited by indigent farmers, yet were also home to recluses who lived in a world of the sublime. People in the small, humble villages of which Lao-tzu spoke were unaware that the Great Way of man lay in living *independently and self-sufficiently, yet they knew this in their hearts. These were the farmers of old. What a tragedy it would be to think of these as fools who know, yet are unaware. To the remark that "any fool can farm," farmers should reply, "a fool cannot be a true farmer." There is no need for philosophy in the farming village. It is the urban intellectual who ponders human existence, who goes in search of truth and questions the purpose of life. The farmer does not wrestle with the questions of why man arose on the face of the earth and how he should live. Why is it that he never learned to question his existence? Life was never so empty and void as to bring him to contemplate the purpose of human existence; there was no seed of uncertainty to lead him astray. With their intuitive understanding of life and death, these farmers were free of anguish and grief; they had no need for learning. They joked that agonizing over life and death, and wandering through ideological thickets in search of truth were the pastimes of idle city youth. Farmers preferred to live common lives, without knowledge or learning. There was no time for philosophizing. Nor was there any need. This does not mean that the farming village was without a philosophy. On the contrary, it had a very important philosophy. This was embodied in the principle that "philosophy is unnecessary." The farming village was above all a society of philosophers without a need for philosophy. It was none other than the philosophy of Mu, or nothingness—which teaches that all is unnecessary, that gave the farmer his enduring strength. Disappearance of the Village Philosophy Not that long ago one could still hear the woodsman sing a woodcutter's song as he sawed down a tree. During transplanting, singing voices rolled over the paddy fields, and the sound of drums surged through the village after the fall harvest. Nor was it that long ago that people used pack animals to carry goods. These scenes have changed drastically over the past twenty years or so. In the mountains, instead of the rasping of hand saws, we now hear the angry snarl of chain saws. We see mechanical plows and transplanters racing over the fields. Vegetables today are grown in vinyl houses ranged in neat rows like factories. The fields are automatically sprayed with fertilizers and pesticides. Because all of the farmer's work has been mechanized and systematized, the farming village has lost its human touch. Singing voices are no longer heard. Everyone sits instead before the TV set, listening to traditional country songs and reminiscing over the past. We have fallen from a true way of life to one that is false. People rush about in a frenzy to shorten time and widen space, and in so doing lose both. The farmer may have thought at first that modern developments would make his job easier. Well, it freed him from the land and now he works harder than ever at other jobs, wearing away his body and mind. The chain saw was developed because someone decided that a tree had to be cut faster. Rather than making things easier for the farmer, the mechanized transplantation of rice has sent him running off to find other work. The disappearance of the sunken hearth from farming homes has extinguished the light of ancient farming village culture. Fireside discussions have vanished, and with them, the village philosophy. High Growth and lhe_Faimin_g Population after World War II No country has' experienced such a sudden and dramatic transformation as Japan following World War II. The country rose rapidly from the ruins of war to become a major economic power. As this was going on, its farming and fishing populations —the seedbed of the Japanese people—fell from fifty percent of the overall population at the end of the war to less than twenty percent today. Without the help of the dexterous, hardworking farmer, the skyscrapers, highways, and subways of the metropolises would never have materialized. Japan owes its current prosperity to the labor it appropriated from the farming population and placed at the service of urban civilization. Japan's rapid growth following the war is generally attributed to good fortune and wise leadership. However, the farmer draws a different interpretation. Changes in the self-image of the farming population led to the adoption of new agricultural methods. As farming became less labor-intensive, surplus manpower poured out of the countryside into the towns and cities, bringing prosperity to the urban civilization. But far from being a blessing, this prosperity has made things harder on the farmer. In effect, he tightened the noose about his own neck. How did this happen? The first step was the arrival of the motorized transport-tiller in the farming village, a major turning point in Japanese agriculture. This was rapidly followed by three-wheeled vehicles and trucks. Before long, ropeways, monorails, and paved roads stretched to the furthest corners of the village, all of which completely altered the farmer's notions of time and space. With this wave of change from labor-intensive to capital-intensive farming came the replacement of the horse-drawn plow with tillers, and later, tractors. Methods of pesticide and fertilizer application underwent major revisions, with motorized hand sprayers being abandoned in favor of helicopter spraying. Needless to say, traditional farming with draft animals was abandoned and replaced with methods involving the heavy application of chemical fertilizers and pesticides. The rapid mechanization of agriculture lit the fires for the revival and precipitous growth of the machine industry, while the adoption of pesticides, chemical fertilizers, and petroleum-based farming materials laid the foundation for development of the chemical industry. It was the desire by farmers to modernize, the sweeping reforms in methods of crop cultivation that opened up the road to a new transformation of society following the destruction of the weapons industry and the industrial infrastructure during the war. What began as a movement to assure adequate food supplies in times of acute shortage grew into a drive to increase food production, the momentum of which carried over into the industrial world. This is where things stood in the mid-1950s. The situation changed completely in the late sixties and early seventies. Stability of food supply had been achieved for the most part and the economy was overflowing with vigor. At last the visions of a modern industrial state were beginning to be realized. It was at about this time that politicians and businessmen started thinking of how to bring the large number of farmers and their land into the picture. Once food surpluses started to arise, the farmers became a weight around the government's neck. The food control system set up to ensure an adequate food supply began to be regarded as a burden on the nation. The Basic Agriculture Law was established in 1961 to define the role and direction to be taken by Japanese agriculture. But instead of serving as a foundation for farmers, it established controls over the farmer and passed the reins of control to the financial community. The general public started thinking that agricultural land could be put to better use in industry and housing than for food production; city dwellers even began to see farmers, who were reluctant to part with their land, as selfish monopolizers of land. Laborers and office workers joined in the effort to drive farmers off their land, and taxes as high as those on housing land were levied on farmland. The effort by farmers to raise food production appears to have backfired against them. Even though Japan's food self-sufficiency has dropped below thirty percent, farmers are unable to speak up because the people of the nation are under the illusion that the farmland reduction policy being pushed through by the government is in the interest of the consumer. Somewhere along the way, the farmer lost both his land and the freedom to choose the crops he wishes to raise. Farmers have simply gone with the flow of the times. Today, most of them lament that they can't make a decent living off farming. Why has the farming community fallen to such a hopeless state? The experience of Japanese farmers over the past 30 years is unprecedented, and poses very grave problems for the future. Let us take a closer look at the fall of Japanese agriculture to determine exactly what happened. How_an_Impoverished National Agricultural Policy Arose When I look closely at the recent history of an agriculture that, unable to oppose the current of the times, has been made to bend and twist to the designs of the leadership, as a farmer, I cannot help feeling tremendous rage. Behind the claim that today's farming youth is being carefully trained as agricultural specialists and model farmers lie plans to wipe out small farms and proposals for a euthanasia of farming. Underlying the spectacular programs for modernizing agriculture and increasing productivity, and the calls to expand the scale of farming operations, lies a thinly-disguised contempt for the farmer. While the one-acre farmer was doing all he could to work his way up to three or even five acres, the policy leaders in government were saying that ten acres just was not large enough, and were running demonstration farms of ISO acres. Clearly, no matter how hard they tried to scale up their operations, farmers were pitted one against another in a fratricidal process of natural selection. To the economists who supported the doctrine of international division of labor, agrarianism and the insistence by farmers that their mission was to produce food were evidence of the obstinate, mule-headed farming temperament which they despised. As for the trading companies, their basic formula for prosperity was to encourage ever more domestic and foreign food trade. Consumers are easily won over by arguments that they have the right to buy cheap, tasty rice. But "tasty" rice is weak rice, polluting rice grown with lots of pesticides. Such demands make things harder on the farmer, and the consumer actually ends up eating bad-tasting rice. The only one who wins out is the merchant. People talk of "cheap rice," but it has never been the farmer who sets the price of rice or other farm produce. Nor is it the farmer who determines production costs. The price of rice nowadays is the price calculated to support the manufacturers of agricultural equipment; it is the price needed for the production of new farm implements; it is the price at which fuel can be bought. When I visited the United States in the summer of 1979, the price of rice on the U.S. market was everywhere about 50 cents per pound—about the same as that of economy rice in Japan. Since the price of gasoline at the time was about one dollar per gallon, I was at a loss to understand the reasoning behind reports then in circulation that rice could easily be imported into Japan at one-quarter to one-third the local price. Just as incredible were reports that the surplus of rice had left the food control system "in the red" or that the scarcity of wheat had kept the system solvent. In natural farming, the cost of producing rice is almost the same as the cost of wheat production. Moreover, both can be produced more cheaply this way than buying imported grain. The mechanism by which the market price of rice is set has nothing whatsoever to do with farmers. The retail price of farm produce is said to be too high in Japan, but this is because the costs of distribution are too high. Distribution costs in Japan are five times those in the United States and twice as high as in West Germany. One cannot help suspecting that the aim of Japan's food policy is to find the best way to line government coffers with gold. The federal assistance given per farmer is twice as high in the United States as in Japan, and three times as high in France. Japanese farmers are treated with indifference. Today's farmers are besieged from all sides. Angry voices rise from the cities, crying: "Farmers are overprotected," "They are over-subsidized," "They're producing too much rice, putting the food control system in debt, and raising our taxes." But these are just the superficial views of people who don't see the whole picture or have any idea of the real state of affairs. I am even tempted to call these false rumors created by the gimmickry of an insanely complex society. At one time, six farming households supported one official. Today, there is reportedly one agriculture or forestry official for every full-time farmer. One wonders then if the agricultural deficits in Japan are really the fault of the farmer. Statistics tell us that the average American farmer feeds one hundred people and the average Japanese farmer only ten, but Japanese farmers actually have a higher productivity than American farmers. It just appears the other way around because Americans farm under much better conditions than Japanese farmers. Farmers today in Japan are in love with money. They no longer have any time or affection for nature or their crops. All they have time for anymore is to blindly follow the figures spit out by distribution industry computers and the plans of agricultural administrators. They don't talk with the land or converse with the crops; they are interested only in money crops. They grow produce without choosing the time or place, without giving a thought to the suitability of the land or crop. The way administrators see it, grain produced abroad and grain grown locally both have the same value. They make no distinction over whether a crop is a short-term or long-term crop. Without giving the slightest thought to the concerns of the farmer, the official instructs the farmer to grow vegetables today, fruits tomorrow, and to forget about rice. However, crop production within the natural ecosystem is no simple matter that can be resolved in an administrative bulletin. It is no wonder then that measures planned from on high are always thwarted and delayed. When the farmer forgets the land to which he owes his existence and becomes concerned only with his own self-interest, when the consumer is no longer able to distinguish between food as the staff of life and food as merely nutrition, when the administrator looks down his nose at farmers and the industrialist scoffs at nature, then the land will answer with its death. Nature is not so kind as to forewarn a humanity so foolish as this. What Lies Ahead for Modern Agriculture In 1979, I boarded a plane for the first time and visited the United States. I was astounded by what I saw. I had thought that desertification and the disappearance of native peoples were stories from ancient history—in the Middle East and Africa. But I learned that the very same thing has happened repeatedly in the U.S. Because meat is the food staple in America, agriculture is dominated by livestock farming. Grazing has destroyed the ecology of natural grasses, devastating the land. I watched this happening and could hardly believe my eyes. Land that has lost its fertility is barren of nature's strength. This accounts for the development of a modern agriculture totally reliant on petroleum energy. The low productivity of the land drives farmers to large-scale operations. Large operations require mechanization with machinery of increasing size. This "big iron" breaks down the structure of the soil, setting up a negative cycle. Agriculture that ignores the forces of nature and relies solely on the human intellect and human effort is unprofitable. It was inevitable that these crops, produced as they are with the help of petroleum, would be transformed into a strategic commodity for securing cheap oil. To get an idea of just how fragile commercial agriculture is with its large-scale, subcontractor-type monoculture farming, just consider that U.S. farmers working 500 to 700 acres have smaller net incomes than Japanese farmers on 3 to 5 acres. I realized, however, that these faults of modern farming were rooted in the basic illusions of Western philosophy that support the foundations of scientific agriculture. I saw that mistaken ideology had led man astray in how he lived his life and secured his essentials of food, clothing, and shelter. I noted that confusion over food had bred confusion over farming, which had destroyed nature. And I understood also that the destruction of nature had enfeebled man and thrown the world into disarray. Is There a Future for Natural Farming? I do not wish merely to expose and attack the current state of modern agriculture, but to point out the errors of Western thought and call for observance of the Eastern philosophy of Mu. While recalling the self-sufficient farming practices and natural diets of the past, my desire has been to establish a natural way of farming for the future and explore the potential for its spread and adoption by others. Yet I suppose that whether natural farming becomes the method of farming for the future depends both on a general acceptance of the thinking on which it is based and on a reversal in the existing value system. Although I will not expound here on this philosophy of Mu and its system of values, I would like to take a brief look at the agriculture of the future from the perspective of Mu. Forty years ago, I predicted that the age of centrifugal expansion fed by the growing material desires of man, the era of rampant modern science, would soon pass and be replaced by a period of contraction and convergence as man sought to improve his spiritual life. I take it that I was wrong. Even organic farming, which has come into its own with the pollution problem, only serves as a temporary stopgap, a brief respite. This is essentially a rehashing of the animal-based traditional farming of the past. Being part and parcel of scientific agriculture to begin with, it will be swallowed whole and assimilated by scientific agriculture. I had hoped that the self-sufficient agriculture of the past and farming methods that try to tap into the natural ecosystem would help turn Japanese thinking around and reorient it toward natural farming—the true way of agriculture, but the current situation is almost behind hope. Science Continues on an Unending Rampage In today's society, man is cut off from nature and human knowledge is arbitrary. To take an example, suppose that a scientist wants to understand nature. He may begin by studying a leaf, but as his investigation progresses down to the level of molecules, atoms, and elementary particles, he loses sight of the original leaf. Nuclear fission and fusion research is among the most advanced and dynamic fields of inquiry today, and with the development of genetic engineering, man has acquired the ability to alter life as he pleases. A self-appointed surrogate of the Creator, he has gotten hold of a magic wand, a sorcerer's staff. And what is man likely to attempt in the field of agriculture? He probably intends to begin with the creation of curious plants by interspecific genetic recombination. It should be easy to create gigantic varieties of rice. Trees will be crossed with bamboo, and eggplants will be grown on cucumber vines. It will even become possible to ripen tomatoes on trees. By transferring genes from leguminous plants to tomato or rice, scientists will produce rhizobium-bearing tomatoes capable of fixing nitrogen from the air. Once tomatoes and rice are developed that do not require nitrogen fertilizer, farmers will no doubt jump at the chance to grow these. Genetic engineering will most certainly be applied to insects as well. If hybrid beeflies are created, or butterfly-dragonflies, we will no longer be able to tell whether these are beneficial insects or pests. Yet, just as the queen ant produces nothing but worker ants, man will try to create any insect or animal that is of benefit to him. Eventually, things may progress to the point where hybrids of foxes and raccoons will be created for zoos, and we may see vegetable-like or mechanical humans created as workers. The most ridiculous products, if developed initially for the sake of medicine, let us say, will receive the plaudits of the world and win wide acceptance. A good example is the recent news, received as a godsend, that the mass production of insulin has been achieved through genetic recombination using E. coli genes. The Illusions of Science and the Farmer Today we have test-tube babies, and scientists are already envisioning a day, not that far off, when they will breed superior humans in culture media by transferring in the genes of gifted physicists and mathematicians. Perhaps they dream of creating new races of men. There will no longer be any need to go through the ordeal of giving birth, or raising children for that matter, as children will be raised in complete incubators equipped with dispensers supplying artificial protein foods and vitamins. No longer will food consist of unappetizing meal protein synthesized from petrochemicals. Instead, we will enjoy delicious, inexpensive meat-like products created by crossing the genes of the soybean with the genes of the cow or pig. Such dreams of science are so close to being achieved, I can see them as if they were already a reality. When that day does come, what will be the role of farmers then? Working the open fields under the sun may become a thing of the past. The farmer may find himself assisting the scientist as a laborer in a tightly sealed factory—perhaps even one for mass-producing strong, intelligent, artificial humans to eliminate the trouble of using or dealing with ordinary human beings. To the scientist, this sort of tragedy appears as but a temporary inconvenience, a necessary sacrifice. Firm and unshaking in his conviction that, while still imperfect, someday human knowledge will be complete, that knowledge is of value as long as it is not put to the wrong use, he will probably continue to rise eagerly to the challenge of empty possibilities. But these dreams of scientists are just mirages, nothing more than wild dancing in the hand of the Lord Buddha. Even if scientists change the living and nonliving as they please and create new life, the fruits and creations of human knowledge can never exceed the limits of the human intellect. In the eyes of nature, actions that arise from human knowledge are all futile. All is arbitrary delusion created by the false reasoning of man in a world of relativity. Man has learned and achieved nothing. He is destroying nature under the illusion that he controls it. Casting and befouling himself as a plaything, he is bringing the earth to the abyss of annihilation. Nor will it be just the farmer who follows the bidding of the scientist and lends him a hand. What a tragedy if this is what awaits the farmer of tomorrow. What a tragedy too for those who laugh at the ruin of each farmer, and those as well who merely look on. All that remains is a last glimmer of hope that the principle dying like a buried ember in the farming village will be unearthed and revived in time to establish a natural way of farming that unites man and nature.*

3
Decline in the Quality of Food

It should have come as no surprise that crops grown with vast amounts of petroleum energy would suffer a decline in quality. The use of oil-based energy in agriculture has gotten to the point where one could almost talk of growing rice in the "oil patch" rather than in the "paddy." Farming under the open skies has disappeared. Agriculture today has been degraded to the manufacture of petroleum-derived foods, and the farmer has become a seller of false goods called "nutritional food." Ever since the farmer who had worked hand in hand with nature capitulated to the pressures of society and became a subcontractor to the oil industry, control over his livelihood has passed into the hands of the industrialist and businessman. Today it is the merchant who has the last say over the farmer's right to loss or gain, life or death. The destruction of agriculture can be seen, for example, in the transition by farmers from the open cultivation of vegetables to hothouse horticulture. This began with the seeding and growing of melons and tomatoes in soil within hot beds or vinyl houses arranged in neat rows. The next stage was sand culture and gravel culture using sand or gravel in place of soil because these materials have fewer bacteria and are thus "cleaner." This was accompanied by a change in thinking—replacing the notion of forming rich soil with that of administering nutrients—-which led to the creation and supply of nutrient solutions. The only function of the sand and gravel was to support the plant, so a simpler, more readily available material was sought. Plastic or polymer netting and containers were developed in which seeds are "planted." As these germinate and grow, the roots extend out in all directions within the plastic netting. The stem and leaves are also artificially supported, and the tightly sealed chamber in which the plants are grown is completely sterile, eliminating the chance, at first, of insect damage or blight. Since the root absorption of nutrients dissolved in water is inefficient, the nutrient solution is sprayed on a regular basis over the entire plant. Nutrients are taken in not only through the roots, but also through leaf surfaces, so they are more immediately available, resulting in a higher growth rate. The temperature is increased and the level of light exposure raised with artificial lighting. Carbon dioxide is sprayed and oxygen pumped in, making plant growth several times faster than in field cultivation. However, any product grown in such an artificial environment is a far cry from products grown under natural conditions. True, freshly colored melons with a beautifully networked skin and a sweet taste and fragrance can be produced, as can large red tomatoes and supple green cucumbers of good texture. But it is a mistake to think of these as good for man. Grown unnaturally as they are, these products are inferior in quality, although perhaps in ways unknown to man. Nature has struck back fiercely against this affront by technology, in the form of increased insect damage. Predictably, the response by man has been an agriculture increasingly dependent on pesticides and fertilizers. Artificial cultivation leads ultimately to the total synthesis of food. The creation of factories for purely chemical food synthesis that will render farms and gardens unnecessary is already underway. This will make of agriculture an activity entirely unrelated to nature. The synthesis of urea has enabled man to produce any organic material he wishes. Protein synthesis enables man-made meat to be fabricated from various materials. Butter and cheese can- be made from petroleum. Sooner or later, as further progress is made in research on photosynthesis, man will surely learn how to synthesize starch. He may even succeed one day in doing this by the saccharification of wood and oil. Man has learned how to synthesize nucleic acid and cellular proteins and nuclei, and is beginning to synthesize and recombine genes and chromosomes. He has even begun thinking that he can control life itself. Not only that. As the notion has settled in that he may soon be able to alter all living things in any way he pleases, man has begun fancying himself as the Creator. Yet all that he learns, all that he performs and creates with science, is a mere imitation of nature and propels him further along the path to suicidal self-destruction. Production Costs Are Not Coming Down It is a mistake to believe that progress in agricultural technology will lower production costs and make food less expensive. Suppose that some entrepreneur decided to grow rice and vegetables in a large building right at the center of a major city. He would make full spatial use of the building in three dimensions, fully equipping it with central heating and air conditioning, artificial lighting, and automatic spraying devices for carbon dioxide and nutrient solutions. Now, would such systemized agriculture involving automated production under the watchful eyes of a single technician really provide people with fresh, inexpensive, and nutritious vegetables? A vegetable factory like this cannot be built and run without considerable outlays for capital and materials, so it is only natural to expect the vegetables thus produced to be expensive. However efficient and modern it may be, such a plant cannot possibly grow produce more cheaply than crops grown naturally with sunlight and soil. Nature produces without calling for supplies or remuneration, but human effort always demands payment in return. The more sophisticated the equipment and facilities, the higher the costs. And man never knows when to stop. When a highly efficient robot is developed, people applaud, saying that efficient production is here at last. But their joy is short-lived, for soon they are dissatisfied again and demanding even more advanced and efficient technology. Everyone seems intent on lowering production costs, yet these costs have skyrocketed nevertheless. Equally mistaken is the notion that food can be produced cheaply and in large quantity with microorganisms such as chlorella and yeast. Science cannot produce something from nothing. Invariably, the result is a decrease in production rather than an increase, giving a high-cost product. People brought up eating unnatural food develop into artificial, anti-natural human beings with an unnatural body prone to disease and an unnatural way of thinking. There exists the frightful possibility that the transfiguration of agriculture may result in the perversion of far more than just agriculture. Increased Production Has Not Brought Increased Yields When talk everywhere turned to increasing food production, most people believed that raising yields and productivity through scientific techniques would enable man to produce larger, better, more plentiful food crops. Yet, larger harvests have not brought greater profits for farmers. In many cases, they have even resulted in losses. Most high-yield farming technology in use today does not increase net profits. At fault are the very practices thought to be vital to increasing yields: the heavy application of chemical fertilizers and pesticides, and indiscriminate mechanization. But although these may be useful in reducing crop losses, they are not effective techniques for increasing productivity. In fact, such practices hurt productivity. They appear to work because: 1) Chemical fertilizers are effective only when the soil is dead. 2) Pesticides are effective only for protecting unhealthy plants.

3) Farm machinery is useful only when one has to cultivate a large area. Another way of saying the same thing is that these methods are ineffective or even detrimental on fertile soil, healthy crops, and small fields. Chemical fertilizers can increase yields when the soil is poor to begin with and produces only 4 to 5 bushels of rice per quarter-acre. Even then, heavy fertilization produces an average rise in yield of not more than about 2 bushels over the long term. Chemical fertilizers are truly effective only on soil abused and wasted through slash-and-burn agriculture. Adding chemical fertilizer to soil that regularly produces 7 to 8 bushels of rice per quarter-acre has very little effect, while addition to fields that yield 10 bushels may even hurt productivity. Chemical fertilizer is thus of benefit only as a means for preventing a decline in yields. Green manure—nature's own fertilizer—and animal manure were cheaper and safer methods of increasing yields. The same is true of pesticides. What sense can there be in producing unhealthy rice plants and applying powerful pesticides anywhere up to ten times a year? Before investigating how well pesticides kill harmful insects and how well they prevent crop losses, scientists should have studied how the natural ecosystem is destroyed by these pesticides and why crop plants have weakened. They should have investigated the causes underlying the disruption in the harmony of nature and the outbreak of pests, and on the basis of these findings decided whether pesticides are really needed or not. By flooding the paddy fields and breaking up the soil with tillers until it hardens to the consistency of adobe, rice farmers have created conditions that make it impossible to raise crops without tilling, and in the process have deluded themselves into thinking this to be an effective and necessary part of farming. Fertilizers, pesticides, and farm machinery all appear convenient and useful in raising productivity. However, when viewed from a broader perspective, these kill the soil and crops, and destroy the natural productivity of the earth. "But after all," we are often told, "along with its advantages, science also has its disadvantages." Indeed, the two are inseparable; we cannot have one without the other. Science can produce no good without evil. It is effective only at the price of the destruction of nature. This is why, after man has maimed and disfigured nature, science appears to give such striking results—when all it is doing is repairing the most extreme damage. Productivity of the land can be improved through scientific farming methods only when its natural productivity is in decline. These are regarded as high-yielding practices only because they are useful in stemming crop losses. To make matters worse, man's efforts to return

conditions to their natural state are always incomplete and accompanied by great waste. This explains the basic energy extravagance of science and technology. Nature is entirely self-contained. In its eternal cycles of change, never is there the slightest extravagance or waste. All the products of the human intellect—which has strayed far from the bosom of nature—and ail man's labors are doomed to end in vain. Before rejoicing over the progress of science, we should lament those conditions that have driven us to depend on its helping hand. The root cause for the decline of the farmer and crop productivity lie with the development of scientific agriculture. Energy-Wasteful Modern Agriculture The claim is often made that scientific agriculture has a high productivity, but if we calculate the energy efficiency of production, we find that this decreases with mechanization. Table 1.1 compares the amount of energy expended directly in rice production using five different methods of farming: natural farming, farming with the help of animals, and lightly, moderately, and heavily mechanized agriculture. Natural farming requires only one man day of labor to recover 130 pounds of rice, or 200,000 kilocalories of food energy, from a quarter-acre of land. The energy input needed to recover 200,000 kilocalories from the land in this way is the 2,000 kilocalories required to feed one farmer for one day. Cultivation with horses or oxen requires an energy input five to ten times as great, and mechanized agriculture calls for an input of from ten to fifty times as much energy. Since the efficiency of rice production is inversely proportional to the energy input, scientific agriculture requires an energy expenditure per unit of food produced up to fifty times that of natural farming. The youths living in the mud-walled huts of my citrus orchard have shown me that a person's minimum daily calorie requirement is somewhere about 1,000 calories for a "hermit's diet" of brown rice with sesame seeds and salt, and 1,500 calories on a diet of brown rice and vegetables. This is enough to do a farmer's work—equivalent to about one-tenth of a horsepower.

At one time, people believed that using horses and oxen would lighten the labor of men. But contrary to expectations, our reliance on these large animals has been to our disadvantage. Farmers would have been better off using pigs and goats to plow and turn the soil. In fact, what they should have done was to leave the soil to be worked by small animals—chickens, rabbits, mice, moles, and even worms. Large animals only appear to be useful when one is in a hurry to get the job done. We tend to forget that it takes over two acres of pasture to feed just one horse or cow. This much land could feed fifty or even a hundred people if one made full use of nature's powers. Raising livestock has clearly taken its toll on man. The reason India's farmers are so poor today is that they raised large numbers of cows and elephants which ate up all the grass, and dried and burned the droppings as fuel. Such practices have depleted soil fertility and reduced the productivity of the land. Livestock farming today is of the same school of idiocy as the fish-farming of yellowtails. Raising one yellowtail to a marketable size requires ten times its weight in sardines. Similarly, a silver fox consumes ten times its weight in rabbit meat, and a rabbit ten times its weight in grass. What an incredible waste of energy to produce a single silver fox pelt! People have to work ten times as hard to eat beef as grain, and they had better be prepared to work five times as hard if they want to nourish themselves on milk and eggs. Farming with the labor of animals therefore helps satisfy certain cravings and desires, but increases man's labor many times over. Although this form of agriculture appears to benefit man, it actually puts him in the service of his livestock. In raising cattle or elephants as members of the farming household, the peasants of Japan and India impoverished themselves to provide their livestock with the calories they needed. Mechanized farming is even worse. Instead of reducing the farmer's work, mechanization enslaves him to his equipment. To the farmer, machinery is the largest domestic animal of all—a great guzzler of oil, a consumer good rather than a capital good. At first glance, mechanized agriculture appears to increase the productivity per worker and thus raise income. However, quite to the contrary, a look at the efficiency of land utilization and energy consumption reveals this to be an extremely destructive method of farming. Man reasons by comparison. Thus he thinks it better to have a horse do the plowing than a man, and thinks it more convenient to own a ten-horsepower tractor than to keep ten horses—why, if it costs less than a horse, a one-horsepower motor is a bargain! Such thinking has accelerated the spread of mechanization and appears reasonable in the context of our currency-based economic system. But the progressively inorganic character and towered productivity of the land resulting from farming operations aimed at large-volume production, the economic disruption caused by the excessive input of energy, and the increased sense of alienation deriving from such a direct antithesis to nature has only speeded the dislocation of farmers off the land, however much this has been called progress. Has mechanization really increased productivity and made things easier for the farmer? Let us consider the changes this has brought about in tilling practices. A two-acre farmer who purchases a 30-horsepower tractor will not magically become a 50-acre farmer unless the amount of land in his care increases. If the land under cultivation is limited, mechanization only lowers the number of laborers required. This surplus manpower begets leisure. Applying such excess energy to some other work increases income, or so the reasoning goes. The problem, however, is that this extra income cannot come from the land. In fact, the yield from the land will probably decrease while the energy requirements skyrocket. In the end, the farmer is driven from his fields by his machinery. The use of machinery may make working the fields easier, but revenue from crop production has shrunk. Yet taxes are not about to decrease, and the costs of mechanization continue to climb by leaps and bounds. This is where things stand for the farmer. The reduction in labor brought about by scientific farming has succeeded only in forcing farmers off the land. Perhaps the politician and consumer think the ability of a smaller number of workers to carry out agricultural production for the nation is indicative of progress. To the farmer, however, this is a tragedy, a preposterous mistake. For every tractor operator, how many dozens of farmers are driven off the land and forced to work in factories making agricultural implements and fertilizer—which would not be needed in the first place if natural farming were used. Machinery, chemical fertilizers, and pesticides have drawn the farmer away from nature. Although these useless products of human manufacture do not raise the yields of his land, because they arc promoted as tools for making profits and boosting yields, he labors under the illusion that he needs them. Their use has wrought great destruction on nature, robbing it of its powers and leaving man no choice but to tend vast fields by his own hand. This in turn has made large machinery, high-grade compound fertilizers, and powerful poisons indispensable. And the same vicious cycle goes on and on without end. Larger and larger agricultural operations have not given farmers the stability they seek. Farms in Europe are ten times larger, and in the United States one hundred times larger, than the 6- to 7-acre farms common to Japan. Yet farmers in Europe and the U.S. are, if anything, even more insecure than Japanese farmers. It is only natural that farmers in the West who question the trend toward large-scale mechanized agriculture have sought an alternative in Eastern methods of organic farming. However, as they have come to realize also that traditional agriculture with farm animals is not the way to salvation, these farmers have begun searching frantically for the road leading toward natural farming. Laying to Waste the Land and Sea The modern livestock and fishing industries are also basically flawed. Everyone unquestioningly assumed that by raising poultry and livestock and by fish farming our diet would improve, but no one had the slightest suspicion that the production of meat would ruin the land and the raising of fish would pollute the seas. In terms of caloric production and consumption, someone will have to work at least twice as hard if he wants to eat eggs and milk rather than grains and vegetables. If he likes meat, he will have to put out seven times the effort. Because it is so energyinefficient, modern livestock farming cannot be considered as "production" in a basic sense. In fact, true efficiency has become so low and man has been driven to such extremes of toil and labor that he is even attempting to increase the efficiency of livestock production by raising large, genetically improved breeds. The Japanese Bantam is a breed of chicken native to Japan. Leave it to roam about freely and it lays just one small egg every other day—low productivity by most standards. But although this chicken is not an outstanding egg-layer, it is in fact very productive. Take a breeding pair of Bantams, let them nest every so often, and before you know it they will hatch a clutch of chicks. Within a year's time, your original pair of chickens will have grown to a flock often or twenty birds that together will lay many times as many eggs each day as the best variety of White Leghorn. The Bantams are very efficient calorie producers because they feed themselves and lay eggs on their own, literally producing something from nothing. Moreover, as long as the number of birds remains appropriate for the space available, raising chickens in this way does not harm the land. Genetically-upgraded White Leghorns raised in cages lay one large egg a day. Because they produce so many eggs, it is commonly thought that raising these in large numbers will provide people with lots of eggs to eat and also generate droppings that can be used to enrich the land. But in order for the chickens to lay so many eggs, they have to be given feed grain having twice the caloric value of the eggs produced. Such artificial methods of raising chickens are thus basically counterproductive; instead of increasing calories, they actually cut the number of calories in half. Restoration of the wastes to the land is not easy, and even then, soil fertility is depleted to the extent of the caloric loss. This is true not only for chickens but for pigs and cattle as well, where the efficiency is even worse. The ratio of energy output to input is 50 percent for broilers, 20 percent for pork, 15 percent for milk, and 8 percent for beef. Raising beef cattle cuts the food energy recoverable from land tenfold; people who eat beef consume ten times as much energy as people on a diet of rice. Few are aware of how our livestock industry, which raises cattle in indoor stalls with feed grain shipped from the United States, has helped deplete American soil. Not only are such practices uneconomical, they amount essentially to a campaign to destroy vegetation on a global scale. Nonetheless, people persist in believing that raising large numbers of chickens that are good egg-layers or improved breeds of hogs and cattle with a high feed conversion efficiency in enclosures is the only workable approach to mass production; they are convinced that this is intelligent, economical livestock farming. The very opposite is true. Artificial livestock practices consisting essentially of the conversion of feed into eggs, milk, or meat are actually very energy-wasteful. In fact, the larger and more highly improved the breed of animal being raised, the greater the energy input required and the greater the effort and pains that must be taken by the farmer. The question we must answer then is: What should be raised, and where? First we must select breeds that can be left to graze the mountain pastures. Raising large numbers of genetically improved Holstein cows and beef cattle in indoor pens or small lots on concentrated feed is a highly risky business for both man and livestock alike. Moreover, such methods yield higher rates of energy loss than other forms of animal husbandry. Native breeds and varieties such as Jersey cattle, which are thought to be of lower productivity, actually have a higher feed efficiency and do not lead to depletion of the land. Being closer to nature, the wild boar and the black Berkshire pig are in fact more economical than the supposedly superior white Yorkshire breed. Profits aside, it would be better to raise small goats than dairy cattle. And raising deer, boars, rabbits, chickens, wildfowl, and even edible rodents, would be even more economical—and better protect nature—than goats. In a small country like Japan, rather than raising large dairy cattle, which merely impoverishes the soil, it would be far wiser for each family to keep a goat. Breeds that are better milk producers but basically weak, such as Saanen, should be avoided and strong native varieties that can live on roughage raised. The goat, which is called the poor man's cattle because it takes care of itself and also provides milk, is in fact inexpensive to raise and does not weaken the productivity of the land. If poultry and livestock are to truly benefit man, they must be capable of feeding and fending for themselves under the open sky. Only then will food become naturally plentiful and contribute to man's well-being. In my idealized vision of livestock farming, I see bees busily making the rounds of clover and vegetable blossoms thickly flowering beneath trees laden heavy with fruit; I see semijwild chickens and rabbits frolicking with dogs in fields of growing wheat, and great numbers of ducks and mallards playing in the rice paddy; at the foot of the hills and in the valleys, black pigs and boars grow fat on worms and crayfish, and from time to time goats peer out from the thickets and trees. This scene might be taken from an out-of-the-way hamlet in a country untarnished by modern civilization. The real question for us is whether to view it as a picture of primitive, economically disadvantaged life or as an organic partnership between man, animal, and nature. An environment comfortable for small animals is also an ideal setting for man. It takes 200 square yards of land to support one human being living on grains, 600 square yards to support someone living on potatoes, 1,500 square yards for someone living on milk, 4,000 square yards for someone living on pork, and 10,000 square yards for someone subsisting entirely on beef. If the entire human population on earth were dependent on a diet of just beef, humanity would have already reached its limits of growth. The world population could grow to three times its present level on a diet of pork, eight times on a milk diet, and twenty times on a potato diet. On a diet of just grains, the carrying, capacity of earth is sixty times the current world population. One need look only at the United States and Europe for clear evidence that beef impoverishes the soil and denudes the earth. Modern fishing practices are just as destructive. We have polluted and killed the seas that were once fertile fishing grounds. Today's fishing industry raises expensive fish by feeding them several times their weight in smaller fish while rejoicing at how abundant fish have become. Scientists are interested only in learning how to make bigger catches or increasing the number of fish, but viewed in a larger context, such an approach merely speeds the decline in catches. Protecting seas in which fish can still be caught by hand should be a clear priority over the development of superior methods for catching fish. Research on breeding technology for shrimp, sea bream, and eels will not increase the numbers of fish. Such misguided thinking and efforts are not only undermining the modern agricultural and fishing industries, they will also someday spell doom for the oceans of the world. As with modern livestock practices that run counter to nature, man has tricked himself into believing that he can improve the fishing industry through the development of more advanced fish farming methods while at the same time perfecting fishing practices that destroy natural reproduction. Frankly, I am frightened at the dangers posed by treating fish with large doses of chemicals to prevent pelagic diseases that break out in the Inland Sea as a result of pollution caused by the large quantities of feed strewn over the water at the many fish farming centers on the Sea. It was no laughing matter when a rise in demand for sardines as feed for yellowtails resulted in a curious development recently: an acute shortage of sardines that made the smaller fish a luxury item for a short while. Man ought to know that nature is fragile and easily harmed. It is far more difficult to protect than everyone seems to think. And once it has been destroyed, nature cannot be restored. The way to enrich man's diet is easy. It does not entail mass growing or gathering. But it does require man to relinquish human knowledge and action, and to allow nature to restore its natural bounty. Indeed, there is no other way.

4

THE ILLUSIONS OF NATURAL SCIENCE

Scientific agriculture developed early in the West as one branch of the natural sciences, which arose in Western learning as the study of matter. The natural sciences took a materialistic viewpoint that interpreted nature analytically and dialectically. This was a consequence of Western man's belief in a man-nature dichotomy. In contrast to the Eastern view that man should seek to become one with nature, Western man used discriminating knowledge to place man in opposition to nature and attempted, from that vantage point, a detached interpretation of the natural world. For he was convinced that the human intellect can cast off subjectivity and comprehend nature objectively. Western man firmly believed nature to be an entity with an objective reality independent of human consciousness, an entity that man can know through observation, reductive analysis, and reconstruction. From these processes of destruction and reconstruction arose the natural sciences. The natural sciences have advanced at breakneck speed, flinging us into the space age. Today, man appears capable of knowing everything about the universe. He grows ever more confident that, sooner or later, he will understand even phenomena as yet unknown. But what exactly does it mean for man to "know"? He may laugh at the folly of the proverbial frog in the well, but is unable to laugh off his own ignorance before the vastness of the universe. Although man, who occupies but one small corner of the universe, can never hope to fully understand the world in which he lives, he persists nonetheless in the illusion that he has the cosmos in the palm of his hand. Man is not in a position to know nature. Nature Must Not Be Dissected Scientific farming first arose when man, observing plants as they grew, came to know these and later grew convinced that he could raise them himself. Yet has man really known nature? Has he really grown crops and lived by the fruit of his own labor? Man looks at a stalk of wheat and says he knows what that wheat is. But does he really know wheat, and is he really capable of growing it? Let us examine the process by which man thinks he can know things. Man believes that he has to fly off into outer space to learn about space, or that he must travel to the moon to know the moon. In the same way, he thinks that to know a stalk of wheat, he must first take it in his hand, dissect it, and analyze it. He thinks that the best way to learn about something is to collect and assemble as much data on it as possible. In his efforts to learn about nature, man has cut it up into little pieces. He has certainly learned many things in this way, but what he has examined has not been nature itself. Man's curiosity has led him to ask why and how the winds blow and the rain falls. He has carefully studied the tides of the sea, the nature of lightning, and the plants an3 animals that inhabit the fields and mountains. He has extended his inquiring gaze into the tiny world of microorganisms, into the realm of minerals and inorganic matter. Even the sub-microscopic universe of molecules, atoms, and subatomic particles has come under his scrutiny. Detailed research has pressed forth on the morphology, physiology, ecology, and every other conceivable aspect of a single flower, a single stalk of wheat. Even a single kaf presents infinite opportunities for study. The collection of cells that together form the leaf; the nucleus of one of these cells, which harbors the mystery of life; the chromosomes that hold the key to heredity; the question of how chlorophyll synthesizes starch from sunlight and carbon dioxide; the unseen activity of roots at work; the uptake of various nutrients by the plant; how water rises to the tops of tall trees; the relationships between various components and microorganisms in the soil; how these interact and change when absorbed by the roots and what functions they serve—these arc but a few of the inexhaustible array of topics scientific research has pursued. But nature is a living, organic whole that cannot be divided and subdivided. When it is separated into two complementary halves and these divided again into four, when research becomes fragmented and specialized, the unity of nature is lost. The diagram in Figure 2.1 is an attempt to illustrate the interplay of factors, or elements, that determine yields in rice cultivation. Originally, the elements determining yield were not divided and separate. All were joined in perfect order under a single conductor's baton and resonated together in exquisite harmony. Yet, when science inserted its scalpel, a complex and horrendously chaotic array of elements appeared. All science has succeeded in doing is to peel the skin off a beautiful woman and reveal a bloody mass of tissue. What a miserable, wasted effort. Nowadays, plants can be made to bloom in all seasons. Stores display fruits and vegetables throughout the year, so that one almost forgets whether it is summer or winter anymore. This is the result of chemical controls that have been developed to regulate the time of bud formation and differentiation. Confident of his ability to synthesize the proteins that make up cells, man has even challenged the "ultimate" secret—the mystery of life itself. Whether he will succeed in synthesizing cells depends on his ability to synthesize nucleic acids, this being the last major hurdle to the synthesis of living matter. The synthesis of simple forms of life is now just a matter of time, this was first anticipated when the notion of a fundamental difference between living and non-living matter was laid to rest with the discovery of bacteriophages, the confirmation—in subsequent research on viral pathogens—of the existence of non-living matter that multiplies, and the first attempts to synthesize such matter. Following his interests blindly, man is intently at work on the synthesis of life without knowing what the successful creation of living cells means or the repercussions it might have. Nor is this all. Carried along by their own momentum, scientists have even begun venturing into chromosome synthesis. Soon after the disclosure that man had synthesized life came the announcement that the synthesis and modification of chromosomes has become possible through genetic recombination. Man can already create and alter living organism:; like the Creator. We are about to enter an age in which scientists will create organisms that have never before appeared on the face of the earth. Following test-tube babies, we will see the creation of artificial beings, monsters, and enormous crops. In fact, these have already begun to appear. Granted, one certainly does get the impression that great advances have be;n made m human understanding, that man has come to know all things in nature and, by using and adapting such knowledge, has accelerated progress in human life. Yet, there is a catch to all of this. Man's awareness is intrinsically imperfect, and this gives rise to errors in human understanding. When man says that he is capable of knowing nature, to "know" does not mean to grasp and understand the true essence of nature. It means only that man knows that nature which he is able to know. Just as the world known to a frog in a well is not the entire world but only the world within that well, so the nature that man can perceive and know is only that nature which he has been able to grasp with his own hands and his own subjectivity. But of course, this is not true nature. The Maze of Relative Subjectivity When people want to know what Okuninushi no Mikoto, the Shinto deity of agriculture, carries around in the huge sack on his shoulder, they immediately open the sack and thrust their hands in. They think that to understand the interior of the sack, they must know its contents. Supposing they found the-sack to be filled with all sorts of strange objects made of wood and bamboo. At this point, most people would begin to make various pronouncements: "Why this no doubt is a tool used by travelers." "No, it's a decorative carving." "No, it most definitely is a weapon." And so forth. Yet the truth, known only to Okuninushi himself, is that the object is an instrument fashioned by him for his amusement. And moreover, because it is broken, he is carrying it around in his sack merely for use as kindling. Man jumps into that great sack called nature, and grabbing whatever he can, turns it over and examines it, asking himself what it is and how it works, and drawing his own conclusions about what purpose nature serves. But no matter how careful his observations and reasoning, each and every interpretation carries the risk of causing grievous error because man cannot know nature any more than he can know the uses for the objects in Okuninushi's sack. Yet man is not easily discouraged. He believes that, even if it amounts to the same absurdity as jumping into the sack and guessing at the objects inside, man's knowledge will broaden without limit; simple observations will start the wheels of reason and inference turning. For example, man may see some shells attached to a piece of bamboo and mistake it for a weapon. When further investigation reveals that rapping the shells against the bamboo makes an interesting sound, he will conclude this to be a musical instrument, and will infer from the curvature of the bamboo that it must be worn dangling from the waist while dancing. With each step in this line of reasoning, he will believe himself that much closer to the truth. Just as he believes that he can know Okuninushi's mind by studying the contents of his sack, so man believes that, by observing nature, he can learn the story of its creation and can in turn become privy to its very designs and purpose. But this is a hopeless illusion, for man can know the world only by stepping outside of the sack and meeting face-to-face with the owner. A flea born and raised in the sack without ever having seen the world outside will never be able to guess that the object in the sack is an instrument that is hung from Okuninushi's belt, no matter how much it studies the object. Similarly, man, who is born within nature and will never be able to step outside of the natural world, can never understand all of nature merely by examining that part of nature around him. Man's answer to this is that, although he may not be able to view the world from without, if he has the knowledge and ability to explore the furthest reaches of the vast, seemingly boundless universe and is able at least to learn what there is and what has happened in this universe, is not this enough? Has not man learned, sooner or later, everything that he wished to learn? That which is unknown today will become known tomorrow. This being the case, there is nothing man cannot know. Even if he were to spend his entire life within a sack, provided he was able to learn everything about the inside of the sack, would this not be enough? Is not the frog in the well able to live there in peace and tranquility? What need has it for the world outside the well? Man watches nature unfold about him; he examines it and puts it to practical use. If he gets the expected results, he has no reason to call into question his knowledge or actions. There being nothing to suggest that he is in error, does not this mean that he has grasped the real truth about the world? He assumes an air of indifference: "I don't know what lies outside the world of the unknown; maybe nothing. This goes beyond the sphere of the intellect. We'd be better off leaving inquiries into a world that may or may not exist to those men of religion who dream of God." But who is it that is dreaming? Who is it that is seeing illusions? And knowing the answer to this, can we enjoy true peace of mind? No matter how deep his understanding of the universe, it is man's subjectivity that holds up the stage on which his knowledge performs. But just what if his subjective view were all wrong? Before laughing at blind faith in God, man should take note of his blind faith in himself. When man observes and judges, there is only the thing called "man" and the thing being observed. It is this thing called "man" that verifies and believes in the reality of an object, and it is man who verifies and believes in the existence of this thing called "man." Everything in this world derives from man and he draws all the conclusions. In which case, he need not worry about being God's puppet. But he does run the risk of acting out a drunken role on the stage supported by the crazed subjectivity of his own despotic existence. "Yes," persists the scientist, "man observes and makes judgments, so one cannot deny that subjectivity may be at work here. Yet his ability to reason enables man to divest himself of subjectivity and see things objectively as well. Through repeated inductive experimentation and reasoning, man has resolved all things into patterns of association and interaction. The proof that this was no mistake lies about us, in the airplanes, automobiles, and all the other trappings of modern civilization." But if, on taking a better look at this modern civilization of ours, we find it to be insane, we must conclude that the human intellect which engendered it is also insane. It is the perversity of human subjectivity that gave rise to our ailing modern age. Indeed, whether one views the modern world as insane or not may even be a criterion of one's own sanity. We have already seen, in Chapter 1, how perverted agriculture has grown. Are airplanes really fast, and cars truly a comfortable way to travel? Isn't our magnificent civilization nothing more than a toy, an amusement? Man is unable to see the truth because his eyes are veiled by subjectivity. He has looked at the green of trees without knowing true green, and has "known" the color crimson without seeing crimson itself. That has been the source of all his errors. Non-Discriminating Knowledge The statement that science arose from doubt and discontent is often used as implied justification of scientific inquiry, but this in no way justifies it, On the contrary, when confronted with the havoc wrought by science and technology on nature, one cannot help feeling disquiet at this very process of scientific inquiry that man uses to separate and classify his doubts and discontents. An infant sees things intuitively. When observed without intellectual discrimination, nature is entire and complete—a unity. In this non-discriminating view of creation, there is no cause for the slightest doubt or discontent. A baby is satisfied and enjoys peace of mind without having to do anything. The adult mentally picks things apart and classifies them; he sees everything as imperfect and fraught with inconsistency. This is what is meant by grasping things dialectically. Armed with his doubts about "imperfect" nature and his discontent, man has set forth to improve upon nature and vainly calls the changes he has brought about "progress" and "development." People believe that as a child grows into adulthood his understanding of nature deepens and through this process he becomes able to contribute to progress and development in this world. That this "progress" is nothing other than a march toward annihilation is clearly shown by the spiritual decay and environmental pollution that plague the developed nations of the world. When a child living in the country comes across a muddy rice field, he jumps right in and plays in the mud. This is the simple, straightforward way of a child who knows the earth intuitively. But a child raised in the city lacks the courage to jump into the field. His mother has constantly been after him to wash the grime from his hands, telling him that dirt is filthy and full of germs. The child who "knows" about the "awful germs" in the dirt sees the muddy rice field as unclean, an ugly and fearful place. Are the mother's knowledge and judgment really better than the unschooled intuition of the country child? Hundreds of millions of microorganisms crowd each gram of soil. Bacteria are present in this soil, but so are other bacteria that kill these bacteria, and yet other bacteria that kill the killer bacteria. The soil contains bacteria harmful to man, but also many that are harmless or even beneficial to man. The soil in the fields under the sun is not only healthy and whole, it is absolutely essential to man. A child who rolls in the din grows up healthy. An unknowing child grows up strong. What 'this means is that the knowledge that "there are germs in the soil" is more ignorant than ignorance itself. People would expect the most knowledgeable person on soil to be the soil scientist. But if, in spite of his extensive knowledge on soil as mineral matter in flasks and test tubes, his research does not allow him to know the joy of lying on the ground under the sun, he cannot be said to know anything about the soil. The soil that he knows is a discreet, isolated part of a whole. The only complete and whole soil is natural soil before it is broken down and analyzed, and it is the infant and child who best know, in their ingenuous way, what truly natural soil is. The mother (science) who parades her partial knowledge implants in the child (modern man) a false image of nature. In Buddhism, knowledge that splits apart self and object and sets them up in opposition is called "discriminating knowledge," while knowledge that treats self and object as a unified whole is called "non-discriminating knowledge," the highest form of wisdom. Clearly, the "discriminating adult" is inferior to the "non-discriminating child," for the adult only plunges himself into ever-deepening confusion.

The Limits to Analytical Knowledge The scientific method consists of four basic steps. The first is to consciously focus one's attention on something and to observe and examine it mentally. The second step is to use one's powers of discernment and reasoning to set up a hypothesis and formulate a theory based on these observations. The third is to empirically uncover a single principle or law from concurring results gathered through analogous experiences and repeated experimentation. And finally, when the results of inductive experimentation have been applied and found to hold, the final step is to accept this knowledge as scientific truth and affirm its utility to mankind. As this process begins with research that discriminates, breaks down, and analyzes, the truths it grasps can never be absolute and universal. Thus scientific knowledge is by definition fragmented and incomplete; no matter how many bits of incomplete knowledge are collected together, they can never form a complete whole. Man believes that the continued dissection and deciphering of nature enable broad generalizations to be made which give a full picture of nature, but this only breaks nature down into smaller and smaller fragments and reduces it to ever greater imperfection. The judgment by man that science understands nature and can use it to create a more perfect world has had the very opposite effect of making nature incomprehensible and has drawn man away from nature and its blessings, so that he now gladly harvests imitation crops far inferior to those of nature. To illustrate, let us consider the scientist who brings a soil sample back to the laboratory for analysis. Finding the sample to consist of organic and inorganic matter, he divides the inorganic matter up into its components, such as nitrogen, potassium, phosphorus, calcium, and manganese, and studies, say, the pathways by which these elements are absorbed by plants as nutrients. He then plants seeds in pots or small test plots to study how plants grow in this soil. He also carefully examines the relationships between microorganisms in the soil and inorganic soil components, and the roles and effects of these microorganisms. The wheat that grows of its own accord from fallen seed on the open ground and the wheat planted and grown in laboratory pots are both identical, but man expends great time, effort, and resources to raise wheat, all because of the blind faith he has in his own ability to grow more and better wheat than nature. Why does he believe this? Wheat growth varies with the conditions under which the wheat is grown. Noting a variation in the size of the heads of wheat, the scientist sets about to investigate the cause. He discovers that when there is too little calcium or magnesium in the soil within the pot, growth is poor and the leaves whither. When he artificially supplements the calcium or magnesium, he notes that the rate of growth increases and large grains form. Pleased with his success, the scientist calls his discovery scientific truth and treats it as an infallible cultivation technique. But the real question here is whether the lack of calcium or magnesium was a true deficiency. What is the basis for calling it a deficiency, and is the remedy prescribed really in the best interests of man? When a field really is deficient in some component, the first thing done should be to determine the true cause of the deficiency. Yet science begins by treating the most obvious symptoms. If there is bleeding, it stops the bleeding. For a calcium deficiency, it immediately applies calcium. If this does not solve the problem, then science looks further and any number of reasons may come to light: perhaps the over-application of potassium reduced calcium absorption by the plant or changed the calcium in the soil to a form that cannot be taken up by the plant. This calls for a new approach. But behind every cause, there is a second and a third cause. Behind every phenomenon there is a main cause, a fundamental cause, an underlying cause, and contributing factors. Numerous causes and effects intertwine in a complex pattern that leaves little clue as to the true cause. Even so, man is confident of the ability of science to find the true cause through persistent and ever deeper investigation and to set up effective ways of coping with the problem. Yet, just how far can he go in his investigation of cause and effect? There Is No Cause-and-Effect in Nature Behind every cause lie countless other causes. Any attempt to trace these back to their sources only leads one further away from an understanding of the true cause. When soil acidity becomes a problem, one jumps to the immediate conclusion that the soil does not contain enough lime. However this deficiency of lime may be due not to the soil itself, but to a more fundamental cause such as erosion of the soil resulting from repeated cultivation on ground exposed by weeding; or perhaps it is related to the rainfall or temperature. Applying lime to treat soil acidity thought to result from insufficient lime may bring about excessive plant growth and increase acidity even further, in which case one ends up confusing cause with effect. Soil acidity control measures taken without understanding why the soil became acidic in the first place may be just as likely to prolong acidity as to reduce it. Right after the war, I used large quantities of sawdust and wood chips in my orchard. Soil experts opposed this, saying that the organic acids produced when the wood rots would most likely make the soil acidic and that to neutralize it I would have to apply large quantities of lime. Yet the soil did not turn acid, so lime was not needed. What happens is that, when bacteria start decomposing the sawdust, organic acids are produced. But as the acidity rises, bacterial growth levels off and molds begin to flourish. When the soil is left to itself, the molds are eventually replaced by mushrooms and other fungi, which break the sawdust down to cellulose and lignin. The soil at this point is neither acidic nor basic, but hovers about a point of equilibrium. The decision to counteract the acidity of rotting wood by applying lime only addresses the situation at a particular moment in time and under certain assumed conditions without a full understanding of the causal relationships involved. Nonintervention is the wisest course of action. The same is true for crop diseases. Believing rice blast to be caused by the infiltration of rice blast bacteria, farmers are convinced beyond a doubt that the disease can be dispelled by spraying copper or mercury agents. However, the truth is not so simple. High temperatures and heavy rainfall may be contributing factors, as may the overapplication of nitrogenous fertilizers. Perhaps flooding of the paddy during a period of high temperature weakened the roots, or the variety of rice being grown has a low resistance to rice blast disease. Any number of interrelated factors may exist. Different measures may be adopted at different times and under different conditions, or a more comprehensive approach applied. But with a general acceptance of the scientific explanation for rice blast disease comes the belief that science is working on a way to combat the disease. Steady improvement in the pesticides used for the direct control of the disease has led to the present state of affairs where pesticides are applied several times a year as a sort of panacea. But as research digs deeper and deeper, what was once accepted as plain and simple fact is no longer clear, and causes cease to be what they appear. For instance, even if we know that excess nitrogenous fertilizer is a cause of rice blast disease, determining how the excess fertilizer relates to attack by rice blast bacteria is no easy matter. If the plant receives plenty of sunlight, photosynthesis in the leaves speeds up, increasing the rate at which nitrogenous components taken up by the roots are assimilated as protein that nourishes the stem and leaves or is stored in the grain. But if cloudy weather persists or the rice is planted too densely, individual plants may receive insufficient light or too little carbon dioxide, slowing photosynthesis. This may in turn cause an excess of nitrogenous components to remain unassimilated in the leaves, making the plant susceptible to the disease. Thus, an excess of nitrogenous fertilizer may or may not be the cause of rice blast disease. One can just as easily ascribe the cause to insufficient sunlight or carbon dioxide, or to the amount of starch in the leaves, but then it turns out that to understand how these factors relate to rice blast disease, we need to understand the process of photosynthesis. Yet modern science has not yet succeeded in fully unlocking the secrets of this process by which starch is synthesized from sunlight and carbon dioxide in the leaves of plants. We know that rotting roots make a plant susceptible to rice blast, but the attempts of scientists to explain why are less than convincing. This happens when the balance between the surface portion of the plant and its roots breaks down. Yet in trying to define what that balance is, we must answer why a weight in-equilibrium in the roots as compared with the stalk and leaves makes the plant susceptible to attack by pathogens, what constitutes an "unhealthy" state, and other riddles that ultimately leave us knowing nothing. Sometimes the problem is blamed on a weak strain of rice, but again no one is able to define what "weak" means. Some scientists talk of the silica content and stalk hardness, while others define "weakness" in terms of physiology, genetics, or some other branch of scientific learning. In the end, we gradually fail to understand even those causes that appeared clear at first, and completely lose sight of the true cause. When man sees a brown spot on a leaf, he calls it abnormal. If he finds an unusual bacteria on that spot, he calls the plant diseased. His confident solution to rice blast disease is to kill the pathogen with pesticides. But in so doing he has not really solved the problem of blast disease. Without a grasp of the true cause of the disease, his solution cannot be a real solution. Behind each cause lies another cause, and behind that yet another. Thus what we view as a cause can also be seen as the result of another cause. Similarly, what we think of as an effect may become the cause of something else. The rice plant itself may see blast disease as a protective mechanism that halts excessive plant growth and restores a balance between the surface and underground portions of the plant. The disease might even be regarded as a means by nature for preventing the overly dense growth of rice plants, thus aiding photosynthesis and assuring the full production of seed. In any case, rice blast disease is not the final effect, but merely one stage in the constant flux of nature. It is both a cause as well as an effect. Although cause and effect may be clearly discernible when observing an isolated event at a certain point in time, if one views nature from a broader spatial and temporal perspective, one sees a tangled confusion of causal relationships that defy unraveling into cause and effect. Even so, man thinks that by resolving this confusion down to its tiniest details and attempting to deal with these details at their most elementary level, he will be able to develop more precise and reliable solutions. But this scientific thinking and methodology only results in the most circuitous and pointless efforts. Viewed up close, organic causal relationships can be resolved into causes and effects, but when examined holistically, no effects and causes are to be found. There is nothing to get ahold of, so all measures are futile. Nature has neither beginning nor end, before nor after, cause nor effect. Causality does not exist. When there is no front or back, no beginning or end, but only what resembles a circle or sphere, one could say that there is unity of cause and effect, but one could just as well claim that cause and effect do not exist. This is my principle of non-causality. To science, which examines this wheel of causality in parts and at close quarters, cause and effect exist. To the scientific mind trained to believe in causality, there most certainly is a way to combat rice blast bacteria. Yet when man, in his myopic way, perceives rice disease as a nuisance and takes the scientific approach of controlling the disease with a powerful bactericide, he proceeds from his first error that causality exists to subsequent errors. From his futile efforts he incurs further toil and misery.

The Laws of Modern Agriculture Certain generally accepted laws have been critical to the development of modern agricultural practices and serve as the foundation of scientific agriculture. These are the laws of diminishing returns, equilibrium, adaptation, compensation and cancellation, relativity, and the law of minimum. I would like to examine here the validity of each from the standpoint of natural farming. But before doing so, a brief description of these laws will help to show why each, when examined by itself, appears to stand up as an unassailable truth. Law of Diminishing Returns: This law states, for example, that when one uses scientific technology to grow rice or wheat on a given plot of land, the technology proves effective up to some upper limit, but exceeding this limit has the reverse effect of diminishing yields. Such a limit is not fixed in the real world; it changes with time and circumstance, so agricultural technology constantly seeks ways to break through it. Yet this law teaches that there are definite limits to returns and that beyond a certain point additional effort is futile. Equilibrium; Nature works constantly to strike a balance, to maintain an equilibrium. When this balance breaks down, forces come into effect that work to restore it. All phenomena in the natural world act to restore and maintain a state of equilibrium. Water flows from a high point to a low point, electricity from a high potential to a low potential. Flow ceases when the surface of the water is level, when there is no longer any difference in the electrical potential. The chemical transformation of a substance stops when chemical equilibrium has been restored. In the same way, all the phenomena associated with living organisms work tirelessly to maintain a state of equilibrium. Adaptation: Animals live by adapting to their environment and crops similarly show the ability to adapt to changes in growing conditions. Such adaptation is one type of activity aimed at restoring equilibrium in the natural world. The concepts of equilibrium and adaptation are thus intimately related and inseparable from each other. Compensation and Cancellation: When rice is planted densely, the plants send out fewer tillers, and when it is planted sparsely, a larger number of stalks grow per plant. This is said to illustrate compensation. The notion of cancellation can be seen, for example, in the smaller heads of grain that result from increasing the number of stalks per plant, or in the smaller grains that form on heads of rice nourished to excessive size with heavy fertilization. Relativity: Factors that determine crop yield are associated with other factors, and all change constantly in relation to each other. An interrelationship exists, for example, between the planting period and the quantity of seed sown, between the time and amount of fertilizer application, and between the number of seedlings and the spacing of plants. No particular amount of seed broadcast, quantity of fertilizer applied, or sowing period is decisive or critical under all conditions. Rather, the fanner constantly weighs one factor against another, making relative judgments that this variety of grain, that method of cultivation, and that type of fertilizer over there is right for such-and-such a period. Law of Minimum: This universally known law, first proposed by Justus von Liebig, a German chemist, may be said to have laid the foundation for the development of modern agriculture. It states that the yield of a crop is determined by the one element, of all those making up the yield, in shortest supply. Liebig illustrated this with a diagram now known as Liebig's barrel. The amount of water—or yield—the barrel holds is determined by that nutrient in shortest supply. No matter how large the supply of other nutrients, it is that nutrient of which there is the greatest scarcity that sets the upper limit on the yield. A typical illustration of this principle would point out that the reason crops fail on volcanic soil in spite of the abundance of nitrogen, potassium, calcium, iron, and other nutrients is the scarcity of phosphates. Indeed, the addition of phosphate fertilizer often results in improved yields. In addition to tackling problems with soil nutrients, this concept has also been applied as a basic tool for achieving high crop yields. All Laws Are Meaningless Each of the above laws is treated and applied independently, yet are these really different and distinct from one another? My conclusion is that nature is an indivisible whole; all laws emanate from one source and return to Mu, or nothingness. Scientists have examined nature from every conceivable angle and have seen this unity as a thousand different forms. Although they recognize that these separate laws are intimately related and point in the same general direction, there is a world of difference between this realization and the awareness that all laws are one and the same. One could read into the law of diminishing returns a force at work in nature that strives to maintain equilibrium by opposing and suppressing gradual increases in returns. Compensation and cancellation are mutually antagonistic. The forces of cancellation act to negate the forces of compensation, by which mechanism nature seeks to maintain a balance. Equilibrium and adaptability are, beyond any doubt, means of protecting the balance, order, and harmony of nature. And if there is a law of the minimum, then there must also be a law of the maximum. In their search for equilibrium and harmony, plants have an aversion not only to nutrient deficiencies, but to deficiencies and excesses of anything. Each one of these laws is nothing other than a manifestation of the great harmony and balance of nature. Each springs from a single source that draws them all together. What has misled man is that, when the same law emanates from a single source in different directions, he perceives each image as representing a different law. Nature is an absolute void. Those who see nature as a point have gone one step astray, those who see it as a circle have gone two steps astray, and those who see breadth, matter, time, and cycles have wandered off into a world of illusion distant and divorced from true nature. The law of diminishing returns, which concerns gains and losses, does not reflect a true understanding of nature—a world without loss or gain. When one has understood that there is no large or small in nature, only a great harmony, the notion of a minimum and a maximum nutrient also is reduced to a petty, circumstantial view. There was never any need for man to set into play his vision of relativity, to get all worked up over compensation and cancellation, or equilibrium and disequilibrium. Yet, agricultural scientists have drawn up elaborate hypotheses and added explanations for everything, leading farming further and further away from nature and upsetting the order and balance of the natural world. Life on earth is a story of the birth and death of individual organisms, a cyclic history of the ascendance and fall, the thriving and failure, of communities. All matter behaves according to set principles—whether we are talking of the cosmic universe, the world of microorganisms, or the far smaller world of molecules and atoms that make up living and nonliving matter. All things are in constant flux while preserving a fixed order; all things move in a recurrent cycle unified by some basic force emanating from one source. If we had to give this fundamental law a name, we could call it the "Dharmic Law That All Things Return to One." All things fuse into a circle, which reverts to a point, and the point to nothing. To man, it appears as if something has occurred and something has vanished, yet nothing is ever created or destroyed. This is not the same as the scientific law of the conservation of matter. Science maintains that destruction and conservation exist side by side, but ventures no further. The different laws of agricultural science are merely scattered images, as seen through the prisms of time and circumstance, of this fundamental law that all things return to one. Because these laws all derive from the same source and were originally one, it is natural that they should fuse together like stalks of rice at the base of the plant. Man might just as well have chosen to group together the law of diminishing returns, the law of minimum, and the law of compensation and cancellation, for example, and refer to these collectively as the "law of harmony." When we interpret this single law as several different laws, are we really explaining more of nature and achieving agricultural progress? In his desire to know and understand nature, man applies numerous laws to it from many different perspectives. As would be expected, human knowledge deepens and expands, but man is sadly deceived in thinking that he draws closer to a true understanding of nature as he learns more about it. For he actually draws further and further away from nature with each new discovery and each fresh bit of knowledge. These laws are fragments cut from the one law that flows at the source of nature. But this is not to say that if reassembled, they would form the original law. They would not. Just as in the tale of the blind men and the elephant in which one blind man touches the elephant's trunk and believes it to be a snake and another touches one of the elephant's legs and calls it a tree, man believes himself capable of knowing the whole of nature by touching a part of it. There are limits to crop yields. There is balance and imbalance. Man observes the dualities of compensation and cancellation, of life and death, loss and gain. He notes nutrient excess and deficiency, abundance and scarcity, and from these observations derives various laws and pronounces them truths. He believes that he has succeeded in knowing and understanding nature and its laws, but what he has understood is nothing more than the elephant as seen by the blind men. No matter how many fragmentary laws extracted from the single unnamed law of nature are collected together, they can never add up to the great source principle. That the nature observed through these laws differs fundamentally from true nature should come as no surprise. Scientific farming based on the application of such laws is vastly different from natural farming, which observes the basic principle of nature. As long as natural farming stands on this unique law, it is guaranteed truth and possesses eternal life. For although the laws of scientific farming may be useful in examining the status quo, they cannot be used to develop better cultivation techniques.

These laws cannot boost rice yields beyond those attainable by present methods, and are useful only in preventing reduced yields. When the farmer asks: "How many rice seedlings should I transplant per square yard of paddy ?" the scientist launches into a long-winded explanation of how the seedling does not increase yields, how compensation and cancellation are at work keeping seedling growth and the number of tillers within a given range to maintain an equilibrium, how too small a number of seedlings may be the limiting factor for yield and too large a number can cause a decline in the harvested grain. At which point, the farmer asks with exasperation: "So what am I supposed to do?" Even the number of seedlings that should be planted varies with the conditions, and yet this has been the subject of endless research and debate. No one knows how many stalks will grow from the seedlings planted in spring, or how this will affect yields in the fall. All one can do is theorize, after the harvest is in, that a smaller number of seedlings would have been better because of the high temperatures that summer, or that the combination of sparse planting and low temperatures were at fault for the low yields. These laws are of use only in explaining results, and cannot be of any help in reaching beyond what is currently possible. A Critical Look at Liebig's Law of Minimum In any discussion of increased production and high yields, the following are generally given as factors affecting yield: Scientific farming pieces together the conditions and factors that make up production, and either conducts specialized research in each area or arrives at generalizations, on the basis of which it attempts to increase yields. The notion of raising productivity by making partial improvements in a number of these factors of production most likely originated with Liebig's thinking, which has played a key role in the development of modern agriculture in the West. According to Liebig's law of minimum, the yield of a crop is determined by that nutrient present in shortest supply. Implicit in this rule is the notion that yield can be increased by improving the factors of production. Going one step further, this can also be understood to imply that, because the worst factor represents the largest barrier to increased yields, significant improvement can be made in the yield by training research efforts on this factor and improving it. Using the analogy of a barrel (Fig. 2.5), Liebig's law states that, just as the level of the water in a barrel cannot rise above the height of the lowest barrel stave, so yields are determined by the factor of production present in shortest supply. In reality, however, this is not the case. Granted, if we break down the crop nutrients and analyze them chemically, we find that these can be divided into any number of components: nitrogen, phosphorus, potassium, calcium, manganese, magnesium, and so on. But to claim that supplying all these factors in sufficient quantity raises yield is dubious reasoning at best. Rather than claiming that this increases yield, we should say only that it maintains yield. A nutrient in short supply decreases yield, but providing a sufficient amount of this nutrient does not increase yield, it merely prevents a loss in yield. Liebig's barrel fails to apply to real-life situations on two counts. First, what holds up the barrel? The yield of a crop is not determined by just one factor; it is the general outcome of all the conditions and factors of cultivation. Thus, before becoming concerned with the effects that the surplus or shortage of a particular nutrient might have, it would make more sense to decide first the extent to which nutrients play a determining role on crop yields. Unless one establishes the limits, coordinates, and domain represented by the factor known as nutrients, any results obtained from research on nutrients break apart in midair. Liebig's barrel is a concept floating in the air. In the real world, yield is composed of innumerable interrelated factors and conditions, so the barrel should be shown on top of a column or pedestal representing these many conditions. As Figure 2.7 shows, yield is determined by various factors and conditions, such as scale of operations, equipment, nutrient supply, and other considerations. Not only is the effect of a surplus or deficiency of any one factor on the yield very small, there is no real way of telling how great this effect is on a scale of one to ten. Then also, the angle of the column or pedestal holding up the barrel affects the tilt of the barrel, changing the amount of water that it can hold. In fact, because the tilt of the barrel exerts a greater influence on the amount of water held by the barrel than the height of the staves, the level of individual nutrients is often of no real significance. The second reason Liebig's barrel analogy does not apply to the real world is that the barrel has no hoops. Before worrying about the height of the staves, we should look at how tightly they are fitted together. A barrel without hoops leaks horribly and cannot hold water. The leakage of water between the barrel staves due to the absence of tightly fastened hoops represents man's lack of a full understanding of the interrelatedness of different nutrients. One could say that we know next to nothing about the true relationships between nitrogen, phosphorus, potassium, and the dozens of other crop nutrients; that no matter how much research is done on each of these, man will never fully understand the organic connections between all the nutrients making up a single crop. Even were we to attempt to fully understand just one nutrient, this would be impossible because we would also have to determine how it relates to all other factors, including soil and fertilizers, method of cultivation, pests, and the weather and environment. But this is impossible because time and space are in a constant state of flux. Not understanding the relationships between nutrients amounts to the lack of a hoop to hold the barrel staves together. This is the situation at an agricultural research center with separate sections devoted to the study of cultivation techniques, fertilizers, and pest control; even the existence of a planning section and a farsighted director will be unable to pull these sections together into an integral whole with a common purpose. The point of all this is simple: as long as Liebig's barrel is constructed of staves representing various nutrients, the barrel will not hold water. Such thinking cannot produce a true increase in yield. Examining and repairing the barrel will not raise the level of the water. Indeed, this can be done only by changing the very shape and form of the barrel. Broad interpretation of Liebig's law of minimum leads to propositions such as "yield can be raised by improving each of the conditions of production," or "defective conditions being the controlling factors of yield, these should be the first to be improved." But these are equally untenable and false. One often hears that yields cannot be increased in a certain locality because of poor weather conditions, or because soil conditions are poor and must first be improved. This sounds very much as if we were talking of a factory where production is the output of components such as raw materials, manufacturing equipment, labor, and capital. When a damaged gearwheel in a piece of machinery slows production in a factory, productivity can soon be restored by repairing the problem. But crop cultivation under natural conditions differs entirely from industrial fabrication in a plant. In farming, the organic whole cannot be enhanced by the mere replacement of parts. Let us retrace the steps of agricultural research and examine the errors committed by the thinking underlying the law of minimum and analytical chemistry. Where Specialized Research Has Gone Wrong Research on crop cultivation began by examining actual production conditions. The goal being to increase production by improving each of these conditions, research efforts were divided initially into specialized disciplines such as tillage and seeding, soil and fertilizers, and pest control As research progressed in each of these areas, the findings were collected together and applied by farmers to boost productivity. Factors identified as having a controlling influence on productivity were targeted as high-priority research topics. Tillage and seeding specialists believe that improvements in these techniques are critical to increasing yields. They see such questions as when, where, and how to seed, and how to plow a field as the first topics research on crop cultivation should address. A fertilizer specialist will tell you: "Keep fertilizing your plants and they'll just keep on growing. If it's high yields you're after, you've got to give your crops a lot of fertilizer. Increased fertilization is a positive way to raise yields." And the pest control specialist will say: "No matter how carefully you grow your crops and how high the yields you're after, if your fields are damaged by a crop disease or an insect pest, you're left with nothing. Effective disease and pest control is indispensable to high-yield production." All such factors appear to help increase production, but the conventional view is that tillage and seeding methods, breeding, and fertilizer application have a direct positive influence on yields, disease and pest damage reduces yields, and weather disasters destroy crops. But are these actually important factors that work independently of each other under natural conditions to set or increase yields? And is there perhaps a range in the degree of importance of these factors? Let us consider natural disasters, which result in extensive crop damage. Gales that occur when the rice is heading and floods coming shortly after transplantation can have a very decisive effect on yields regardless of the combination of production factors. However, the damage is not the same everywhere. The effects of a single gale can vary tremendously depending on the time and place. In a single stretch of fields, some of the rice plants will have lodged while others will remain standing; some heads of rice will be stripped clean, others will have less than a quarter of the grains remaining, and yet others more than three-quarters. Some rice plants submerged under flood waters will soon recover and continue growing, while others in the same waters will rot and die. Damage may have been light because a host of interrelated factors—seed variety, method of cultivation, fertilizer application, disease and pest control—combined to give healthy plants that were able to recover as growth conditions and the environment returned to normal. Even inclement weather or a natural disaster is intimately and inseparately tied in with other production factors. So it is a mistake to think that any one factor can act independently to override all other factors and exert a decisive effect on yield. This is true also for disease and pest damage. Twenty-percent crop damage by rice borers does not necessarily mean a twenty-percent decline in harvested grain. Yields may actually rise in spite of pest damage. If a farmer expecting twenty-percent crop damage by leaf hoppers in his fields forgoes the use of pesticides, he may find the damage to be effectively contained by the appearance of vast numbers of spiders and frogs that prey on the leafhoppers. Insect damage arises from a number of causes. If we trace each of these back, we find that the damage attributable to any one cause is generally very insignificant. Natural farming takes a broad view of this tangle of causality and the interplay of different factors, and chooses to grow healthy crops rather than exercise pest control. Breeding programs have sought to develop new high-yield strains that are easy to grow, resistant to insect pests and disease, and so on. But the creation and abandoning over the past several decades of tens of thousands of new varieties shows that the goals set for these change constantly, an indication that the question of seed variety cannot be resolved independently of other factors. Although breeding techniques may be useful in achieving temporary gains in yield and quality, such gains are never permanent or universal. The same is triK for methods of cultivation. Undeniable as it is that plowing, the time and period of seeding, and the raising of seedlings are basic to growing crops, we are wrong to think that the skill applied to these methods is decisive in setting yields. Deep plowing was for a long time considered an important factor in determining crop yield, yet today a growing number of farmers no longer believe plowing to be necessary. Some even think that intertillage, weeding, and transplantation, all practices held to be of central importance by most farmers, are not needed at all. The use of such practices is dictated by the thinking of the times and other factors. Another pitfall is the belief that fertilizers and methods of fertilizer application are directly linked to improved yields. Damage by heavy fertilization can just as easily lead to reduced yields. No single factor of production is powerful enough by itself to determine the yield or quality of a harvest. All are closely interrelated and share responsibility with many other factors for the harvest. The moment that he applied discriminating knowledge to his study of nature, the scientist broke nature into a thousand pieces. Today, he picks apart the many factors that together contribute to the production of a crop, and studying each factor independently in specialized laboratories, writes reports on his research which he is confident, when studied, will help raise crop productivity. Such is the state of agricultural science today. While such research helps throw some light on current farming practices and may be effective in preventing a decline in productivity, it does not lead to discoveries of how to raise productivity and achieve spectacularly high yields. Far from benefitting agricultural productivity, progressive specialization in research actually has the opposite effect. Methods intended to boost productivity lead instead to the devastation of nature, lowering overall productivity. Science labors under the delusion that the accumulated findings of an army of investigators pursuing specialized research in separate disciplines will provide a total and complete picture of nature. Although parts may be broken off from the whole, "the whole is greater than the sum of the parts," as the saying goes. By implication, a collection of an infinite number of parts includes an infinite number of unknown parts. These may be represented as an infinite number of gaps, which prevent the whole from ever being completely reassembled. Scientific agriculture believes that by applying specialized research to parts of the whole, partial improvements can be made which will translate into overall improvement of the whole. But nature should not forever be picked apart. Man has become so absorbed in his pursuit of the parts that he has abandoned his quest for the truth of the whole. Or perhaps, inevitably, his attempt to know the parts has made him lose sight of the whole. Fragmented research only produces results of limited utility. All scientific farming can provide are partial improvements that may give high yields and increased production under certain conditions, but these tenuous "gains" soon fall victim to the violent recuperative backlash of nature and never ultimately result in higher yields. Being limited and imperfect, human knowledge cannot hope to win out over the whole and ever-perfect wisdom of nature. Hence, all efforts to raise productivity founded on human knowledge can enjoy only limited success. While they may help deter a decline in yields by compensating for an irregular dip in productivity, such efforts will never be a means for significantly boosting productivity. Although man may interpret the result as an increase in yield, his efforts can never amount to anything more than a means for staving off reduced yields. All of which goes to show that, try as he may, man cannot equal the yields of nature. Critique- of the Inductive and Deductive Methods Scientific thought is founded on inductive and deductive reasoning, so a critical review of these methods will allow us to examine the basic foundations of science. As my example, I will use the process of conducting research on rice cultivation. One normally begins by drawing up a general proposition from a number of facts or observations. Let us say that a comprehensive study of rice is made. To determine the most suitable quantity of rice seed to be sown, the scientist experiments with a variety of seeding quantities. To establish the optimal spacing of plants, he runs tests in which he varies the number of days seedlings are grown in a nursery, and the number and spacing of transplanted seedlings. He compares several different varieties and selects those that give the highest yields. And to set guidelines for fertilizer application, he tries applying different amounts of nitrogen, phosphorus, and potassium. Inferences drawn from the results of these tests form the basis for selecting suitable techniques and quantities to be used in all methods of producing rice. The scientist or farmer, as the case may be, relies on these conclusions to make general decisions and erect standards that he believes help improve rice cultivation. But do a number of disparate improvements add up to the best overall result? This problem lies behind the notable failure of most research to achieve higher yields in rice cultivation. Respective ten-percent improvements through new varieties of rice, tilling and seeding techniques, fertilization, and pest and disease control might be expected to add up to an overall increase of forty percent in yields, but actual improvements in the field amount to from two to ten percent, at best. Why do 1 + 1 + 1 not make 3, but 1? For the same reason that the pieces of a broken mirror can never be reassembled into a mirror more perfect than the original. The reason agricultural research stations were unable to produce more than 15-20 bushels per quarter-acre until around 1965 was that all they were doing, essentially, was to analyze and interpret rice that yielded 15-20 bushels per quarter-acre to begin with. Although such research was launched to develop high-yielding techniques that are more productive than those used by the ordinary farmer, its only achievement has been the addition of scientific commentary on existing rice-growing methods. It has not improved farmer's yields. Such is the fate of inductive research. Scientific agriculture first conducts research primarily by an inductive, or a posteriori, process, then does an about-face, applying deductive reasoning to draw specific propositions from general premises. Natural farming arrives at its conclusions by applying deductive, or a priori, reasoning based on intuition. By this, I do not mean the imaginative formulation of wild hypotheses, but a mental process that attempts to reach a broad conclusion through intuitive understanding. During this process, it draws narrow conclusions adapted to the time and place, and searches out concrete methods in keeping with these conclusions. Natural farming thus begins by formulating conclusions, then seeks concrete means of attaining these. This contrasts sharply with the inductive approach, whereby one studies the situation as it stands and from this derives a theory with which one searches for a conclusion while making gradual improvements along the way. In the first case, we have a conclusion, but no means of achieving it, and in the second, we have means at our disposal, but no conclusion. Returning again to our original example, natural farming uses intuitive reasoning to draw up an ideal vision of rice cultivation, infers the environmental conditions under which a situation approximating the ideal can arise, and work* out a means of achieving this ideal. On the other hand, scientific farming studies all aspects of rice production and conducts many different tests in an attempt to develop increasingly economical and highyielding methods office cultivation. Such inductive experimentation is done without a clear goal. Scientists run experiments oblivious to the direction in which their research takes them. They may be pleased with the results and confident that the amassing of new data leads to steady progress and scientific achievement. But in the absence of a clear goal by which to set their course, this activity is just aimless wandering. It is not progress. The scientist is well aware of the restrictive and circumstantial nature of inductive research, and does give some thought to deductive reasoning. But he ends up relying on the inductive approach because this leads more directly to practical and certain success and achievement. Deductive experimentation has never had much appeal to scientists because they are unable to get a good handle on what appears to many a whimsical process. In addition, as this requires a great deal of time and space, it runs counter to the natural inclinations of scientists, who like to hole up in their laboratories. The reality is that both the inductive and the deductive method thread their way through the entire history of agricultural development. Of the two, deductive reasoning has always been the driving force behind rapid leaps in development, which are invariably triggered by some oddball idea dreamed up by an eccentric or a zealous farmer bit by curiosity. Generally lacking scope and universality, such an idea tends to slide back into oblivion unless the scientist recognizes it as a clue. After taking it apart and analyzing, studying, reconstructing, and verifying it through inductive experimentation, the scientist raises the idea to the level of a universally applicable technique. It is only at this point that the original idea is ready to be put to practical use and may, as often is the case, eventually become widely adopted by farmers. Thus, although the guiding force of agricultural development is inductive reasoning by the scientist, the initial inspiration that lays the rails for progress is often the deductive notion of a progressive farmer or a hint left by someone who has nothing to do with farming. Clearly then, the inductive method is useful only in a negative sense, as a means for preventing a decline in crop yields. Although throwing light on existing methods, it cannot break new ground in agriculture. Only deductive reasoning can bring forth fresh ideas having the potential of leading to positive gains in yields. Yet, because deductive reasoning generally remains poorly understood and is defined primarily in relation to induction, it is not likely to lead to any dramatic increases in yield. True deduction originates at a point beyond the world of phenomena. It arises when one has acquired a philosophical understanding of the true essence of the natural world and grasped the ultimate goal. All that man sees is a superficial image of nature. Unable to perceive the ultimate goal, he assumes deduction to be merely the inverse of induction and can go no further than deductive reasoning, which is but a dim shadow of true deduction. Experiments in which deduction is treated as the counterpart of induction have brought us the confusion of modern science. Even in agriculture, farmers and scientists are confounding measures for preventing crop losses with means for raising yields, and by discussing both on equal terms, are only prolonging the current stagnation of agriculture. Induction and deduction can be likened to two climbers ascending a rock face. The lower of the two, who checks his footing before giving the climber in the lead a boost, plays an inductive role, while the lead climber, who lets down a rope and pulls the lower climber up, plays a deductive role. Induction and deduction are complementary and together form a whole. Surprising as it may seem, although scientific agriculture has relied primarily on inductive experimentation, progress has been made as well in deductive reasoning. This is why measures to prevent crop losses and measures to boost yields have been confused. Deduction here being merely a concept defined in relation to induction, we may see a gradual increase in yields, but are unlikely to see a dramatic improvement. Our two climbers make only slow progress and will never go beyond the peak they have already sighted. To attain dramatically improved yields of a type possible only by a fundamental revolution in farming practices, one would have to rely not on this restricted notion of deduction, but on a broader deductive method; namely, intuitive reasoning. In addition to our two climbers with a rope, other radically different methods of reaching the top of the mountain are possible, such as descending onto the peak by rope from a helicopter. It is from just such intuitive reasoning, which goes beyond induction and deduction that the thinking underlying natural farming arises. The creative roots of natural farming lie in true intuitive understanding. The point of departure must be a true grasp of nature gained by fixing one's gaze on the natural world that extends beyond actions and events in one's immediate surroundings. An infinitude of yield-improving possibilities lie hidden here. One must look beyond the immediate. High-Yield Theory Is Full of_ Holes It is easy for us to think that scientific farming, which harnesses the forces of nature and adds to this human knowledge, is superior to natural farming both from the standpoint of economics and crop yields. This is not the case, of course, for a number of reasons. 1. Scientific farming has isolated the factors responsible for yield and found ways to improve each of these. But although science can break nature down and analyze it, it cannot reassemble the parts into the same whole. What may appear to be nature reconstructed is just an imperfect imitation that can never produce higher yields than natural farming. 2. What is trumpeted as high-yield theory and technology amounts to nothing more than an attempt to approach natural harvests. Rather than aiming at large jumps in yields, as is claimed, these are really just measures to stave off crop losses. 3. Not only does the endeavor to artificially achieve high yields that surpass natural output only increase the level of imperfection, it invites a breakdown in agriculture. Viewed in a larger sense, this is just so much wasted effort. Yields that outstrip nature can never be achieved.

1. Yield is determined by the size of the building and the degree to which each room is full. 2. The upper limit of yield is set by the natural environment, represented here by the strength of the rock foundation and the size of the building site. One could have gotten a reasonably close idea of the potential yield from the blueprints of the building. The limit became fixed when the frame for the building was put into place. This maximum yield may be called the natural yield and is, for man, the best and highest yield. 3. The actual harvest is much lower than this maximum yield, for the harvest does not completely fill each and every room. If the building were a hotel, this would be equivalent to saying that some guest rooms are vacant. In other words, there are invariably flaws or weaknesses in some of the elements of cultivation; these hold down yields. The actual harvest is what we are left with after subtracting the vacant rooms from the total number of guest rooms. 4. The approach usually taken by scientific farming to boost yields is to fill as many of the rooms as possible. But in a larger sense, this is merely a way of minimizing losses in yield. The only true way to raise yields is to enlarge the building itself. 5. Any attempt to outdo nature, to increase production by purely industrial methods that brazenly disregard the natural order, is analogous to adding an annex onto the building representing nature. If we imagine this annex to be built on sand, then we can begin to understand the precariousness of artificial endeavors to raise yields. Inherently unstable, these do not represent true production and do not really benefit man. 6. Although one would assume that filling each of the rooms would reduce losses and produce a net increase in yield, this is not necessarily so because all the rooms are closely interconnected. One cannot make selective improvements here and there in specific factors of production. Knowing all this, we can better comprehend what the building signifies. To accept the thinking of Liebig is to say that yield is dominated by that element present in shortest supply. Such reasoning implies that, if one is not applying enough fertilizer or is using the wrong method of pest control, then correcting this will raise yields. Yet half-baked improvements of this sort are no more effective than renovating just the fourth floor, or just one room on the first floor. The reason is that there are no absolute criteria with which to judge whether one element or condition is good or bad, excessive or insufficient. The qualitative and quantitative aspects of an element vary in a continuously fluid relationship with those of other elements; at times these work together, at other times they cancel each other out. Because he is nearsighted, what man takes to be improvements in various elements are just localized improvements—like remodeling one room of the hotel. There is no way of knowing what effect this will have on the entire building. One cannot know how business is faring at a hotel just by looking at the number of guest rooms or the number of vacancies. True, there may be many empty rooms, but other rooms may be packed full; in some cases, one good patron may be better for business than a large number of other guests. Good conditions in one room do not necessarily have a positive effect on overall business, and bad conditions on the first floor do not always exert a negative influence on the second and third floors. All the rooms and floors of the building are separate and distinct, yet all are intimately linked together into one organic whole. Although one can claim that the final yield is determined by the combination of an infinite array of factors and conditions, just as a new company president can dramatically change morale within the company, so the entire yield of a crop may turn on a change in a single factor. In the final analysis, one cannot predict which element or factor will help or hurt the yield. This can only be determined by hindsight—after the harvest is in. A farmer might say that this year's good harvest was due to the early-maturing variety he used, but he cannot be certain about this because of the unlimited number of factors involved. He has no way of knowing whether using the same variety the following year will again give good results. One could even go to the extreme of saying that the effects of all the factors on the final yield can hinge, for example, on how a typhoon blows. This could turn bad conditions into good conditions. Last year's crop failure might have been the result of spreading too much fertilizer, which led to excessive plant growth and pest damage, but this year is windier so the fertilizer may succeed if the wind helps keep the bugs off the plants. We cannot predict what will work and what will not, so there is no reason for us to be so concerned about minor improvements. Just as the manager of our hotel will never succeed if all he pays attention to is whether the lights in the guest rooms are on or off, careful attention to tiny, insignificant details will never get the farmer off to a good start. Clearly, the only positive way to increase yields is to increase the capacity of the hotel. What we need to know is whether the hotel can be renovated, and if so, how. We must not forget that as the scientist makes additions and repairs and the building gets higher and higher, it becomes increasingly unstable and imperfect. His observations, experiences, and ideas being entirely derived from nature, man can never build a house that extends beyond the bounds of nature. But heedless of this and not content with crops in their natural state, he has broken away from the natural arrangement of environmental factors and begun building an addition to the house of nature—artificially cultivated crops. This artificial, chemically produced food unquestionably presents a dreadful danger to man. More than just a question of wasted effort and meaningless toil, it is the root of a calamity that threatens the very foundations of human existence. Yet agriculture continues to move rapidly toward the purely chemical and industrial production of agricultural crops, an addition——to return to my original analogy—built by man which projects out from the cliff on which nature stands. The side view of the building shows which path to follow in climbing from floor to floor while meeting the requirements for each of the factors of production. For example, since Course 1 begins under poor weather and land conditions, the yield is poor regardless of special efforts invested in cultivation and pest control. Weather and land conditions in Course II are good, so the yield is high even though the method of cultivation and overall management leave something to be desired. One cannot predict, however, which pathway will give the highest yield as there are an infinite number of these, and infinite variations in the factors and conditions for each. While no doubt of use to the theorist for expounding the principles of crop cultivation, this diagram has no practical value. A Look at Photosynthesis: Research aimed at high rice yields likewise begins by analyzing the factors underlying production. This commences with morphological observation, proceeds next to dissection and analysis, then moves on to plant ecology. By conducting laboratory experiments, pot tests, and small-scale field experiments under highly selective conditions, scientists have been able to pinpoint some of the factors that limit yields and some of the elements that increase harvests.

Yet clearly, any results obtained under such special conditions can have little relevance with the incredibly complex set of natural conditions at work in an actual field. It comes as no surprise then that research is turning from the narrow, highly focused study of individual organisms to a broader examination of groups of organisms and investigations into the ecology of rice. One line of investigation being taken to find a theoretical basis for high yields is the ecological study of photosynthetic crops that increase starch production. Many scientists continue to feel, however, that ecological research aimed at increasing the number of heads or grains of rice on a plant, or at providing larger individual grains, are crude and elementary. These people believe that physiological research which lays bare the mechanism of starch production is higher science; they subscribe to the illusion that such revelations will provide a basic clue to high yields. To the casual observer, the study of photosynthesis within the leaves of the rice plant appears to be a research area of utmost importance, the findings of which could lead to a theory of high yields. Let us take a look at this research process. If one accepts that increased starch production is connected to high yields, then research on photosynthesis does take on a great importance. Moreover, as efforts are made to increase the amount of sunlight received by the plant and research is pursued on ways of improving the plant's capacity for starch synthesis from sunlight, people begin thinking that high yields are possible. Current high-yield theory, as seen from the perspective of plant physiology, says essentially that yields may be regarded as the amount of starch produced by photosynthesis in the leaves of the plant, minus the starch consumed by respiration. Proponents of this view claim that yields can be increased by maximizing the photosynthetic ability of the plant while maintaining a balance between starch production and starch consumption. But is all this theorizing and effort useful in achieving dramatic increases in rice yields? The fact of the matter is that today, as in the past, a yield of about 22 bushels per quarter-acre is still quite good, and the goal agronomists have set for themselves is raising the national average above this level. The possibility of reaping 26 to 28 bushels has recently been reported by some agricultural test centers, but this is only on a very limited scale and does not make use of techniques likely to gain wide acceptance. Why is it that such massive and persistent research efforts have failed to bear fruit? Perhaps the answer lies in the physiological process of starch production by the rice plant and in the scientific means for enhancing the starch productivity of the plant.1) The leaves of the plant use photosynthesis to synthesize starch, which the leaves, stem, and roots consume during the process of respiration. 2) The plant produces starch by taking up water through the roots and sending it to the leaves, where photosynthesis is carried out using carbon dioxide absorbed through the leaf stomata and sunlight. 3) The starch produced in the leaves is broken down to sugar, which is sent to all parts of the plant and further decomposed by oxidation. This degradative process of respiration releases energy that feeds the rice plant. 4) A large portion of the starch produced in this way is metabolized by the plant and the remainder stored in the grains of rice. Armed with a basic understanding of how photosynthesis works, the next thing science does is to study ways in which to raise starch productivity and increase the amount of stored starch. Countless factors affect the relative activities of photosynthesis and respiration. Here are some of the most important: Factors affecting photosynthesis: carbon dioxide, stomata closure, water uptake, water temperature, sunlight. Factors affecting respiration: sugar, oxygen, strength of wind, nutrients, humidity. One way of raising rice production that immediately comes to mind here is to maximize starch production by increasing photosynthesis while at the same time holding starch consumption down to a minimum in order to leave as much unconsumed starch as possible in the heads of rice. Conditions favorable for high photosynthetic activity are lots of sunlight, high temperatures, and good water and nutrient uptake by the roots. Under such conditions, the leaf stomata remain open and much carbon dioxide is absorbed, resulting in active photosynthesis and maximum starch synthesis. There is a catch to this, unfortunately. The same conditions that favor photosynthesis also promote respiration. Starch production may be high, but so is starch consumption, and hence these conditions do not result in maximum starch storage. On the other hand, a low starch production does not necessarily mean that yields will be low. In fact, if starch consumption is low enough, the amount of stored starch may even be higher—meaning higher yields—than under more vigorous photosynthetic activity. How often have farmers and scientists tried techniques that maximize starch production only to find the result to be large rice plants that lodge under the slightest breeze? A much easier and more certain path to high yields would be to hold down respiration and grow smaller plants that consume less starch. The combinations of production factors and elements that can occur in nature are limitless and may lead to any number of different yields. Various pathways are possible in Fig. 2.13. For example, when there is abundant sunlight and temperatures are high—around 40°C (104°F), as in Course 1, root rot tends to occur, reducing root vitality. This weakens water uptake, causing the plant to close its stomata to prevent excessive loss of water. As a result, less carbon dioxide is absorbed and photosynthesis slows down, but because respiration continues unabated, starch consumption remains high, resulting in a low yield. In Course 2, temperatures are lower—perhaps 30°C (86°F), and better suited to the variety of rice. Nutrient and water absorption are good, so photosynthetic activity is high and remains in balance with respiration. This combination of factors gives the highest yield. In Course 3, low temperatures prevail and the other conditions are fair but hardly ideal. Yet, because good root activity supplies the plant with ample nutrients, a normal yield is maintained.This is just a tiny sampling of the possibilities, and I have made only crude guesses at the effects several factors on each course might have on the final yield. But in the real world yields are not determined as simply as this. An infinite number of paths exist, and each of the many elements and conditions during cultivation change, often on a daily basis, over the entire growing season. This is not like a footrace along a clearly marked track that begins at the starting line and ends at the finish line. Even were it possible to know what conditions maximize photosynthetic activity, one would be unable to design a course that assembles a combination of the very best conditions. The best conditions cannot be combined under natural circumstances. And to make matters even worse, maximizing photosynthesis does not guarantee maximum yields; nor do yields necessarily increase when respiration is minimized. To begin with, there is no standard by which to judge what "maximum" and "minimum" are. One cannot flatly assert, for example, that 40°C is the maximum temperature, and 30°C optimal. This varies with time and place, the variety of rice, and the method of cultivation. We cannot even know for certain whether a higher temperature is better or worse. Another reason why we cannot know is that the notion of what is appropriate differs for each condition and factor. People are usually satisfied with an optimal temperature that is workable under the greatest range of conditions. Although this answers the most common needs and will help raise normal yields, it is not the temperature required for high yields. Our inquiry into what temperatures are needed for high yields thus proves fruitless and we settle in the end for normal temperatures. What about sunlight? Sunlight increases photosynthesis, but an increase in sunlight is not necessarily accompanied by a rise in yield. In Japan, yields are higher in the northern part of Honshu than in sunny Kyushu to the south, and Japan boasts better yields than countries in the southern tropics. Everyone is off in search of the optimal amount of sunlight, but this varies in relation with many other factors. Good water uptake invigorates photosynthesis, but flooding the field can hasten root decay and slow photosynthesis. A deficiency in soil moisture and nutrients may at times help to maintain root vigor, and may at other times inhibit growth and bring about a decline in starch production. It all depends on the other conditions. An understanding of rice plant physiology can be applied to a scientific inquiry into how to maximize starch production, but this will not be directly applicable to actual ricegrowing operations. Scientific visions of high yields based on the physiology of the rice plant amount to just a lot of empty theorizing. Maybe the numbers add up on paper, but no one can build a theory like this and get it to work in practice. The rice scientist wellversed in his particular specialty is not unlike the sports commentator who can give a good rundown of a tennis match and may even make a respectable coach, but is not himself a top-notch athlete. This inability of high-yield theory to translate into practical techniques is a basic inconsistency that applies to all scientific theory and technology. The scientist is a scientist and the farmer a farmer and "never the twain shall meet." The scientist may study farming, but the farmer can grow crops without knowing anything about science. This is borne out nowhere better than in the history of rice cultivation. Look Beyond the Immediate Reality: Obviously, productivity and yields are measured in relative terms. A yield is high or low with respect to some standard. In seeking to boost productivity, we first have to define a starting point relative to which an increase is to be made. But do we not in fact always aim to produce more, to obtain higher yields, while believing all the while that no harm can come of simply moving ahead one step at a time? When people discuss rice harvests, for some reason they are usually most concerned with attempts to increase yields. By "high-yielding" all we really mean is higher than current rice yields. This might be 20 bushels per quarter-acre in some cases, and over 25 bushels in others. There is no set target for "high-yielding" cultivation. The point of departure defines the destination, and a starting line makes sense only when there is a finish line. Without a starting line we cannot take off. So it is meaningless to talk of great or small, gain or loss, good or bad. Because we take the present for granted as certain and unquestionable reality, we normally make this our point of departure and view as desirable any conditions or factors of production that improve on it. Yet the present is actually a very shaky and unreliable starting point. A good hard look at this so-called reality shows the greater part of it to be man-made, to be erected on commonsensical notions, with all the stability of a building erected on a boat. Taking any one of the traditional notions of rice cultivation—plowing, starter beds, transplantation, flooded paddies—as our basic point of departure would be a grave error. Indeed, true progress can be had only by starting out from a totally new point. But where is one to search for this starting point? I believe that it must be found in nature itself. Yet philosophically speaking, man is the only being that does not understand the true state of nature. He discriminates and grasps things in relative terms, mistaking his phenomenological world for the true natural world.

He sees the morning as the beginning of a new day; he takes germination as the start in the life of a plant, and withering as its end. But this is nothing more than biased judgment on his part. Nature is one. There is no starting point or destination, only an unending flux, a continuous metamorphosis of all things. Even this may be said not to exist. The true essence of nature then is "nothingness." It is here that the real starting point and destination are to be found. To make nature our foundation is to begin at "nothing" and make this point of departure our destination as well; to start off from "nothing" and return to "nothing." We should not make conditions directly before us a platform from which to launch new improvements. Instead, we must distance ourselves from the immediate situation, and observing it at a remove— from the standpoint of Mu, seek to return to Mu nature. This may seem very difficult, but may also appear very easy because the world beyond immediate reality is actually nothing more than the world as it was prior to human awareness of reality. A look from afar at the total picture is no better than a look up close at a small part because both are one inseparable whole. This undivided and inseparable unity is the "nothingness" that must be understood as it is. To start from Mu and return to Mu, that is natural farming. If we strip away the layers of human knowledge and action from nature one by one, true nature will emerge of itself, A good look at the natural order thus revealed will show us just how great have been the errors committed by science. A science that rejects the science of today will surely ensue. Crops need only be entrusted to the hand of nature. The starting point of natural farming is also its destination, and the journey in-between. One may believe the productivity of natural farming—which has no notion of time or space—to be quantifiable or unquantifiable; it makes no difference. Natural farming merely provides harvests that follow a fixed, unchanging orbit with the cycles of nature. Yet, let there be no mistake about it, natural harvests always give the best possible yields; they are never inferior to the harvests of scientific farming. The scientific world of "somethingness" is smaller than the natural world of "nothingness." No degree of expansion can enable the world of science to arrive at the vast, limitless world of nature. Original Factors Are Most Important: We have seen that resolving production into elements or constituent factors and studying ways of improving these individually is basically an invalid approach. Now I would like to examine the propriety of scientists ignoring correlations between different factors, of their adherence to a sliding scale of importance in factors, and of their selective study of those elements that offer the greatest chances for rapid and visible improvement in yields. The factors involved in production are infinite in number, and all are organically interrelated. None exerts a controlling influence on production. Moreover, these cannot and should not be ranked by importance. Each factor is meaningful in the tangled web of interrelationships, but ceases to have any meaning when isolated from the whole. In spite of this, individual factors are extracted and studied in isolation all the time. Which is to say that research attempts to find meaning in something from which it has wrested all meaning. There are commonly thought to be a number of important topics that should be addressed, and factors that should be studied, in order to boost crop production. Since people feel that the quickest way to raise production is to make improvements in those factors thought to be deficient in some way (Liebig's law of minimum), they sow seed, apply fertilizer, and control disease and insect damage. So it comes as no surprise when research follows suit by focusing on methods of cultivation, soil and fertilizers, disease and insect pests. Environmental factors such as climate that are far more difficult for man to alter are given a wide berth. But judging from the results, the factors most critical to yields are not those which man believes he can easily improve, but rather the environmental factors abandoned by man as intractable. Furthermore, it is precisely those factors that we break down, meticulously categorize, and view as vital and important that are the most trivial and insignificant. Those primitive, unresolved factors not yet subjected to the full scrutiny of scientific analysis are the ones of greatest importance. The fact that agricultural research centers are divided into different sections breeding, cultivation, soil and fertilizers, plant diseases and pests—is proof that agricultural research does not take a comprehensive approach to the study of nature. Instead, it starts from simple economic concerns and proceeds wherever man's desires take him, with the result that fragmented research is conducted in response to the concerns of the moment, almost as if by impulse. Whichever field of inquiry we look at—plant breeders who chase after rare and unusual strains; agronomics and its preoccupation with high yields; soil science based on the premise of fertilizer application; entomologists and plant pathologists who devote themselves entirely to the study of pesticides for controlling diseases and pests without ever giving a thought to the role played by poor plant health; and meteorologists who perform token research in agricultural meteorology, a marginal and very narrowly defined discipline that only gets any attention when there is no other alternative—one thing is clear: modern agricultural research is not an attempt to gain a better understanding of the relationship between agricultural crops and man. From beginning to end, this has consisted exclusively of limited, inconsequential analytic research on isolated crops that does not set as its goal an understanding of the interrelationships between man and crops in nature. As research grows increasingly specialized, it advances into ever more narrowly defined disciplines and penetrates into ever smaller worlds. The scientist believes that his studies reach down to the deepest stratum of nature and his efforts bring man that much closer to a fundamental understanding of the natural world, but these endeavors are just peripheral research that moves further and further away from the fountainhead of nature. Early man rose with the sun and slept on the ground. In ancient times, the rays of the sun, the soil, and the rains raised the crops; people learned to live by this and were grateful to the heavens and earth. The man of science is well versed in small details and confident that he knows more about growing crops than the farmer of old. But does the scientist—who is aware that starch is produced within the leaf by photosynthesis from carbon dioxide and water with the aid of chlorophyll, and that the plant grows with the energy released by the oxidation of this starch—know more about light and air than the farmer who thinks the rice has ripened by the grace of the sun? Certainly not! The scientist knows only one aspect, only one function of light and air—that seen from the perspective of science. Unable to perceive light and air as broadly changing phenomena of the universe, man isolates these from nature and examines them in cross-section like dead tissue under a microscope. In fact, the scientist, unable to see light as anything other than a purely physical phenomenon, is blind to light. The soil scientist explains that crops are not raised by the earth, but grow under the effects of water and nutrients, and that high yields can be obtained when these are applied at the right time in the proper quantity. But he should also know that what he has in his laboratory is dead, mineral soil, not the living soil of nature. He should know that the water which flows down from the mountains and into the earth differs from the water that runs over the plains as a river; that the fluvial waters which give birth to all forms of life, from microorganisms and algae to fish and shellfish, are more than just a compound of oxygen and hydrogen. Farmers build greenhouses and hot beds where they grow vegetables and flowers without knowing what sunlight really is or bothering to take a close look at how light changes when it passes through glass or vinyl sheeting. No matter how high a market price they fetch, the vegetables and flowers grown in such enclosures cannot be truly alive or of any great value. No Understanding of Causal Relationships: The farmer might talk about how this year's poor harvest was due to the poor weather, while the specialist will go into more detail: "Tiller formation was good this year resulting in a large number of heads. Grain count per head was also good, but insufficient sunlight after heading slowed maturation, giving a poor harvest." The second explanation is far more descriptive and appears closer to the real truth. Surely one reason for poor maturation is insufficient sunshine, since the two clearly are causally related. Yet one cannot make the claim that a lack of sunlight during heading was the decisive factor behind the poor harvest that year. This is because the causal relationship between these two factors—maturation and sunlight—is unclear. Insufficient sunlight and poor maturation mean that not enough sunlight was received by the leaves. The cause for this may have been drooping of the leaves due to excessive vegetative growth, and the drooping may have been caused by any number of factors. Perhaps this was a result of the over application and absorption of nitrogenous fertilizers, or a shortage of some other nutrient. Perhaps the cause was stem weakness due to a deficiency of silica, or maybe the leaf droop was caused merely by an excess of leaf nitrogen on account of inhibition, for some reason, of the conversion of nitrogenous nutrients to protein. Behind each cause lies another cause. When we talk of causes, we refer to a complex web of organically interrelated causes—basic causes, remote causes, contributing factors, predisposing factors. This is why one cannot give a brief, simple explanation of the true cause of poor maturation, and it is also why a more detailed explanation is no closer to grasping the real truth. The poor harvest might be attributed to insufficient sunshine or to excess nitrogen during heading or merely to poor starch transport due to inadequate water. Or perhaps the basic cause is low temperatures. In any event, it is impossible to tell what the real cause is. So what do we do? The conclusion we draw from all this is that the poor harvest resulted from a combination of factors, which is no more meaningful than the farmer saying it was written in the stars. The scientist may be pleased with himself for coming up with a detailed explanation, but it makes not the slightest bit of difference whether we carefully analyze the reasons for the poor harvest or throw all analysis to the winds; the result is the same. Scientists think otherwise, however, believing that an analysis of one year's harvest will benefit rice growers the following year. Yet the weather is never the same, so the rice growing environment next year will be entirely different from this year's. And because all factors of production are organically interrelated, when one factor changes, this affects all other factors and conditions. What this means is that rice will be grown under entirely different conditions next year, rendering this year's experience and observations totally useless. Although useful for examining results in retrospect, the explanations of yesterday cannot be used to set tomorrow's strategy. The causal relationships between factors in nature are just too entangled for man to unravel through research and analysis. Perhaps science succeeds in advancing one slow step at a time, but because it does so while groping in total darkness along a road without end, it is unable to know the real truth of things.

This is why scientists are pleased with partial explications and see nothing wrong with pointing a finger and proclaiming this to be the cause and that the effect. The more research progresses, the larger the body of scholarly data grows. The antecedent causes of causes increase in number and depth, becoming incredibly complex, such that, far from unraveling the tangled web of cause and effect, science succeeds only in explaining in ever greater detail each of the bends and kinks in the individual threads. There being infinite causes for an event or action, there are infinite solutions as well, and these together deepen and broaden to infinite complexity. To resolve the single matter of poor maturation, one must be prepared to resolve at the same time elements in every field of study that bears upon this—such as weather, the biological environment, cultivation methods, soil, fertilizer, disease and pest control, and human factors. A look at the prospects of such a simultaneous solution should be enough to make man aware of just how difficult and fraught with contradiction this endeavor is. Yet, in a sense, this is already unavoidable. Many people believe that if you take a variety of rice which bears large heads of grain, grow it so that it receives lots of sunlight, apply plenty of fertilizer, and carry out thorough pest control measures, you will get good yields. However, varieties that bear large heads usually have fewer heads per plant. Thus it will do no good to plant densely if the intention is to allow better exposure to sunlight. Moreover, the heavy application of fertilizers will cause excessive vegetative growth, again defeating attempts to improve exposure to sunlight. Efforts to obtain large stems and heads only weaken the rice plant and increase disease and insect damage, while thorough pest control measures result in lodging of the rice plants. The use of water-conserving rice cultivation to improve light exposure of the rice plants may actually cut down the available light due to the growth of weeds, and the lack of sufficient water may even interfere with the transport of nutrients. An attempt to raise the efficiency of photosynthesis may lower the photosynthetic ability of the plant. If we then conclude that irrigation is beneficial for the rice plants and try irrigating, just when high temperatures would be expected to encourage vigorous growth, root rot sets in, resulting in poor maturation. In other words, while a means of improving photosynthesis may prove effective at increasing the amount of starch, it does not necessarily exe^t a beneficial influence on those other elements that help set harvest yields and is in fact more likely to .have countless negative effects. In short, there is no way to join all these into one overall method that works just right. The more improvement measures are combined, the more these measures cancel each other out to give an indefinite result, so that the only conclusion ends up being no clear conclusion at all. If what people have in mind is that a plant variety that bears in abundance, is easy to raise, and has a good flavor would solve everything, they are in for a long wait. The day will never come when one variety satisfies all conditions. The breeding specialist may believe that his endeavors will produce a variety that meets the needs of his age, but an improved variety with three good features will also have three bad features, and one with six strengths will have six weaknesses. All of which goes to show that any variety thought to be better will probably be worse, because in it will lie new contradictions that defy solution. Although when examined individually, each of the improvements conceived by agricultural scientists may appear fine and proper, when seen collectively they cancel each other out and are totally ineffective. This property of mutual cancellation derives from the equilibrium of nature. Nature inherently abhors the unnatural and makes every effort to return to its true state by discarding human techniques for increasing harvests. For this reason, a natural control operates to hold down large harvests and raise low harvests, such as to approach the natural yield without disrupting the balance of nature. In any case, since the basic causes of actions and effects that arise at any particular time and place cannot be known to man, and he can have no true understanding of the causal relationships involved, there is no way for him to know the true effectiveness of any of his techniques. Although he knows that no grand conclusion is forthcoming in the long run, man persists nevertheless in the belief that his partial conclusions and devices are effective in an overall sense. It is utterly impossible to predict what effects will arise from actions undertaken using the human intellect. Man only thinks the effects will be beneficial. He cannot know. Although it would be desirable to erect comprehensive measures and simultaneously apply methods complete on all counts, only God is capable of doing this. As the correlations and causal relationships between all the elements of nature remain unclear, man's understanding and interpretation can at best be only myopic and uncertain. After having succeeded only in causing meaningless confusion, his efforts thus cancel each other out and are eventually buried in nature.

5

Ways of Natural Farming

Although I have already shown in some detail the differences between natural farming and scientific farming, I would like to return here to compare the principles on which each is based. For the sake of convenience, I shall divide natural farming into two types and consider each separately. Mahayana Natural Farming: When the human spirit and human life blend with the natural order and man devotes himself entirely to the service of nature, he lives freely as an integral part of the natural world, subsisting on its bounty without having to resort to purposeful effort. This type of farming, which I shall call Mahayana natural farming, is realized when man becomes one with nature, for it is a way of farming that transcends time and space and reaches the zenith of understanding and enlightenment. This relationship between man and nature is like an ideal marriage in which the partners together realize a perfect life without asking for, giving, or receiving anything of each other. Mahayana farming is the very embodiment of life in accordance with nature. Those who live such a life are hermits and wise men. Hinayana Natural Farming: This type of farming arises when man earnestly seeks entry to the realm of Mahayana farming. Desirous of the true blessings and bounty of nature, he prepares himself to receive it. This is the road leading directly to complete enlightenment, but is short of that perfect state. The relationship between man and nature here is like that of a lover who yearns after his loved one and asks for her hand, but has not realized full union. Scientific Farming: Man exists in a state of contradiction in which he is basically estranged from nature, living in a totally artificial world, yet longs for a return to nature. A product of this condition, scientific farming forever wanders blindly back and forth, now calling upon the blessings of nature, now rejecting it in favor of human knowledge and action. Returning to the same analogy, our lover here is unable to decide whose hand to ask in marriage, and, while agonizing over his indecision, imprudently courts the ladies, heedless of social proprieties. Absolute World Mahayana natural farming (philosopher's way of farming) = pure natural farming Relative World Hinayana natural farming (idealistic farming) = natural farming, organic farming Scientific farming (dialectical materialism) = scientific agriculture The Three Ways of Farming Compared: These may be arranged as above or depicted in the manner.

1. Mahayana natural farming: This and scientific farming are on entirely different planes. Although it is a bit strange to directly compare the two and discuss their relative merits, the only way we have of expressing their value in this world of ours is by comparison and contrast. Scientific agriculture draws as much as it can from natural forces and attempts, by adding human knowledge, to produce results that eclipse nature. Naturally, proponents of this type of farming think it superior to natural farming, which relies entirely on the forces and resources of nature. Philosophically, however, scientific farming cannot be superior to Mahayana natural farming because, while scientific farming is the sum of knowledge and forces extracted from nature by the human intellect, this still amounts to finite human knowledge. No matter how one totals it up, human knowledge is but a tiny, closely circumscribed fraction of the infinitude of the natural world. In contrast to the vast, boundless, perfect knowledge and power of nature, the finite knowledge of man is always limited to small pockets of time and space. Inherently imperfect as it is, human knowledge can never be collected together to form perfect knowledge. As imperfection can never be the equal of perfection, so scientific farming must always yield a step to Mahayana natural farming. Nature encompasses everything. No matter how desperately he struggles, man will never be more than a small, imperfect part of its totality. Clearly then, scientific farming, which is inherently incomplete, can never hope to attain the immutable absoluteness of natural farming. 2. Hinayana natural farming: This type of farming belongs in the same world of relativity as scientific farming, and so the two may be directly compared. Both are alike in that they are derived from that nature which is verified with discriminating knowledge. But Hinayana farming attempts to cast off human knowledge and action and devote itself to making the greatest possible use of the pure forces of nature, whereas scientific farming uses the powers of nature and adds human knowledge and action in an effort to establish a superior way of farming. The two differ

fundamentally and are diametrically opposed in their perceptions, thinking, and the direction of research, but to explain the methods of Hinayana farming we have no choice but to borrow the terms and methods of science. So for the sake of simplicity, we shall place it temporarily in the realm of science. In this respect, it resembles the position of the Eastern arts of healing vis-à-vis Western medicine. The direction in which Hinayana natural farming points leads beyond the world of science and to a rejection of scientific thinking. Borrowing an analogy from the art of sword fighting, Hinayana natural farming may be likened to the one-sword school that is directed toward the center, and scientific farming to the two-sword school that is directed outward. The two can be compared. But Mahayana natural farming is the unmoving no-sword school, comparison with which is impossible. Scientific farming uses all possible means at its disposable, increasing the number of swords, whereas natural farming tries to obtain the best possible results while rendering all means useless, in effect reducing the number of its swords (Hinayana) or doing entirely without (Mahayana). This view is based on the philosophical conviction that if man makes a genuine effort to approach nature, then even should he abandon all deeds and actions, nature will take each of these over and perform them for him. 3. Scientific farming: Pure natural farming should therefore be judged on philosophical grounds, while scientific farming should be evaluated on scientific grounds. Because scientific farming is limited to immediate circumstances in every respect, its achievements may excel in a restricted sense but are invariably inferior in all other ways. In contrast, natural farming is total and comprehensive, so its achievements must be judged from a broad, universal perspective. When scientific methods are used to grow a fruit tree, for example, the goal may be to produce large fruit, in which case all efforts will be concentrated to this end. Yet all that will be achieved is the production of what may, in a limited sense, be regarded as large fruit. The fruit produced by scientific farming is always large—even unnaturally so—in a relative sense, but invariably has grave flaws. Essentially, what is being grown is deformed fruit. To determine the true merit of scientific farming, one has to decide whether producing large fruit is truly good for man. The answer to this should be obvious. Scientific farming constantly practices the unnatural without the slightest concern, but this is of very great significance and invites the gravest of consequences. The unnaturalness of scientific farming leads directly to incompleteness, which is why its results are always distorted and at best of only local utility.

Scientific farming and Hinayana natural farming both occupy the same dimension and may be described as "circles" of equal diameter, although one large difference is the very irregular contour of scientific farming. The irregular shape of scientific farming represents the distortions and imperfections arising from the collection of narrow research findings of which it is made. This contrasts sharply with the perfect circle that signifies the perfection of nature toward which Hinayana natural farming aspires. Because the nature seen by man is just a superficial image of true nature, the circle representing Hinayana farming is drawn much smaller than that for Mahayana natural farming. Mahayana farming, which is nature itself, is superior in every respect to the other ways of farming.

Scientific Agriculture: Farming without Nature Constant changes in crop-growing practices and the shifting history of sericulture and livestock farming show that while man may have approached natural farming in some ages, he leaned more toward scientific agriculture in others. Farming has repeatedly turned back to nature, then moved away again. Today, it is headed toward fully automated and systemized production. The immediate reason for this trend toward mechanized agriculture is that artificial methods of raising livestock and scientific crop cultivation are believed to give higher yields and to be more economically advantageous, meaning higher productivity and profits. Natural farming, on the other hand, is seen as a passive and primitive way of farming, at best a laissez-faire form of extensive agriculture that gives meager harvests and paltry profits. Here is how I compare the yields for these three types of farming: 1) Scientific farming excels under unnatural, man-made conditions. But this is only because natural farming cannot be practiced under such conditions. 2) Under conditions approaching those of nature, Hinayana natural farming will yield results at least as good as or better than scientific farming. 3) In holistic terms, Mahayana natural farming, which is both pure and perfect, is always superior to scientific farming. Let us take a look at situations in which each of these excels. 1. Cases Where Scientific Farming Excels: Scientific methods will always have the upper hand when growing produce in an unnatural environment and under unnatural conditions that deny nature its full powers, such as accelerated crop growth and cultivation in cramped plots, clay pots, hothouses, and hotbeds. And through adroit management, yields can be increased and fruit and vegetables grown out of season to satisfy consumer cravings by pumping in lots of high technology in the form of chemical fertilizers and powerful disease and pest control agents, bringing in unheard-of profits. Yet this is only because under such unnatural conditions natural farming does not stand a chance. Instead of being satisfied with vegetables and fruit ripened on the land under the full rays of the sun, people vie with each other to buy limp, pale, out-of-season vegetables and splendid-looking fruit packed with artificial coloring the minute these appear in the supermarkets and food stalls. Under the circumstances, it is no surprise that people are grateful for scientific farming and think of it as beneficial to man. Yet even under such ideal conditions, scientific farming does not produce more at lower cost or generate higher profits per unit area of land or per fruit tree than natural farming. It is not economically advantageous because it produces more and better product with less work and at lower cost. No, it is suited rather to the skillful use of time and space to create profit. People construct buildings on high-priced land and raise silkworms, chickens, or hogs. In the winter they grow tomatoes and watermelons hydroponically in large hothouses. Mandarin oranges, which normally ripen in late autumn, are shipped from refrigerated warehouses in the summer and sold at a high profit. Here scientific agriculture has the entire field to itself. The only response possible to a consumer public that desires what nature cannot give it is to produce crops in an environment divorced from nature and to allow technology that relies on human knowledge and action to flex its muscle. But I repeat, viewed in a larger sense that transcends space and time, scientific farming is not more economical or productive than natural farming. This superiority of scientific farming is a fragile, short-lived thing, and soon collapses with changing times and circumstances. 2. Cases Where Both Ways of Farming Are Equally Effective: Which of the two approaches is more productive under nearly natural conditions such as field cropping or the summer grazing of livestock? Under such circumstances, natural farming will never produce results inferior to scientific agriculture because it is able to take full advantage of nature's forces. The reason is simple: man imitates nature. No matter how well he thinks he knows rice, he cannot produce it from scratch. All he does is take the rice plant that he finds in nature and tries growing it by imitating the natural processes of rice seeding and germination. Man is no more than a student of nature. It is a foregone conclusion that were nature—the teacher—to use its full powers, man—the student—would lose out in the confrontation. A typical response might go as follows: "But a student sometimes catches up with and overtakes his teacher. Isn't it possible that man may one day succeed in fabricating an entire fruit. Even if this isn't identical to a natural fruit, but just a mere imitation, might it not possibly be better than the real thing?" But has anyone actually given any thought to how much scientific knowledge, to the materials and effort, it would take to reproduce something of nature? The level of technology that would be needed to create a single persimmon seed or leaf is incomparably greater than that used to launch a rocket into outer space. Even were man to undertake a solution to the myriad mysteries in the persimmon seed and attempt to fabricate a single seed artificially, the world's scientists pooling all their knowledge and resources would not be up to the task. And even supposing that this were possible, if man then set his mind on replacing current world fruit production with fruit manufactured in chemical plants that rely solely on the faculties of science, he would probably fall short of his goal even were he to cover the entire face of the earth with factories. I may appear to be overstating the case here, yet man constantly goes out of his way to commit such follies. Man today knows that planting seeds in the ground is much easier than going to the trouble of manufacturing the same seeds scientifically. He knows, but he persists in such reveries anyway. An imitation can never outclass the original. Imperfection shall always lie in the shadow of perfection. Even though man is well aware that the human activity we call science can never be superior to nature, his attention is riveted on the imitation rather than the original because he has been led astray by his peculiar myopia that makes science appear to excel over nature in certain areas. Man believes in the superiority of science when it comes to crop yields and aesthetics, for example. He expects scientific farming, with its use of high-yielding techniques, to provide richer harvests than natural farming. He is convinced that taller plants can be grown by spraying hormones on rice plants grown under the forces of nature; that the number of grains per head can be increased by applying fertilizer during heading; that higher-than-natural yields can be attained by applying any of a host of yield-enhancing techniques. Yet, no matter how many of these disparate techniques are used together, they cannot increase the total harvest of a field. This is because the amount of sunlight a field receives is fixed, and the yield of rice, which is the amount of starch produced by photosynthesis in a given area, depends on the amount of sunlight that shines on that area. No degree of human tampering with the other conditions of rice cultivation can change the upper limit in the rice yield. What man believes to be high-yielding technology is just an attempt to approach the limits of natural yields; more accurately, it is just an effort to minimize harvest losses. So what is man likely to do? Recognizing the upper limit of yields to be set by the amount of sunlight the rice plants receive, he may well try to breach this barrier and produce yields higher than naturally possible by irradiating the rice plants with artificial light and blowing carbon dioxide over them to increase starch production. This is certainly possible in theory, but one must not forget that such artificial light and carbon dioxide are modeled on natural sunlight and carbon dioxide. These were created by man from other materials and did not arise spontaneously. So it is all very well and good to talk of additional increases in yield achieved over the natural limits of production by scientific technology, but because such means require enormous energy outlays they are not true increases. Even worse, man must take full responsibility for destruction of the cyclic and material order of the natural world brought about by the use of technology. Since this disruption in the balance of nature is the basic cause of environmental pollution, . man has brought lengthy suffering down upon his own head. The Entanglement of Natural and Scientific Farming As I mentioned earlier, natural farming and scientific farming are diametrically opposed. Natural farming moves centripetally toward nature, and scientific farming moves centrifugally away from nature. Yet many people think of these two approaches as being intertwined like the strands of a rope, or see scientific farming as repeatedly moving away from nature, then returning back again, something like the in-and-out motion of a piston. This is because they believe science to be intimately and inseparably allied with nature. But such thinking does not stand on a very firm foundation. The paths of nature and of science and human action are forever parallel and never cross. Moreover, because they proceed in opposite directions, the distance between nature and science grows ever larger. As it moves along its path, science appears to maintain a cooperative association and harmony with nature, but in reality it aspires to dissect and analyze nature to know it completely in and out. Having done so, it will discard the pieces and move on without looking back. It hungers for struggle and conquest. Thus, with every two steps forward that science takes, it moves one step back, returning to the bosom of nature and drinking of its knowledge. Once nourished, it ventures again three or four steps away from nature. When it runs into problems or out of ideas, it returns, seeking reconciliation and harmony. But it soon forgets its debt of gratitude and begins again to decry the passiveness and inefficiency of nature. Let us take a look at an example of this pattern as seen in the development of silkworm cultivation. Sericulture first arose when man noticed the camphor si!k moth and the tussah spinning cocoons in mountain forests and learned that silk can be spun from these cocoons. The cocoons are fashioned with silk threads by moth larvae just before they enter the pupal stage. Having studied how these cocoons are made, man was no longer satisfied with just collecting natural cocoons and hit upon the idea of raising silkworms to make cocoons for him. Primitive methods close to nature are believed to have marked the beginnings of sericulture. Silkworms were collected and released in woods close to home. Eventually man replaced these wild species with artificially bred varieties. He noticed that silkworms thrive on mulberry leaves and that, when young, they grow more rapidly if these leaves are fed to them finely chopped. At this point, it became easier to raise them indoors, so he built shelves that allowed him to grow large numbers of worms inside. He devised feeding shelves and special tools for cocoon production, and became very concerned about optimum temperature and humidity. The methods used during this long period of sericulture development demanded a great deal of hard labor from farming households. One had to get up very early in the morning, shoulder a large basket, and walk out to the mulberry grove, there to pick the leaves one at a time. The leaves were carefully wiped free of dew with dry cloths, chopped into strips with a large knife, and scattered over the silkworms on the tens and hundreds of feeding shelves. The grower carefully maintained optimum conditions night and day, taking the greatest pains to adjust room temperature and ventilation by installing heaters and opening and closing doors. He had no choice; the silkworms improved by artificial breeding were weak and susceptible to disease. It was not uncommon for the worms, after having finally grown to full size, to be suddenly wiped out by disease. During spinning of the silk from the cocoons, all the members of the family pitched in, rarely getting any sleep. Growing and care of the mulberry trees also kept farmers busy with fertilizing and weeding. If a late frost killed the young leaves, then one usually had no choice but to throw away the whole lot of silkworms. Given such labor-intensive methods, it should come as no surprise then that people began to look for less strenuous techniques. Starting 15 to 20 years ago, sericulture techniques that approach natural farming spread widely among growers. These methods consisted of, for example, throwing branches of mulberry leaves onto the silkworms rather than picking and chopping leaves. Once it was learned that such a crude method works for young silkworms as well as the fully grown larvae, the next thought that occurred to growers was that, instead of raising the worms in a special room, they might perhaps be raised outdoors in a small shed, under the eaves, or in a sort of hotbed. On trying the idea out, growers found that silkworms are really quite hardy and never had to be raised under constant temperature and humidity conditions. Needless to say, they were overjoyed. Originally a creature of nature, the silkworms thrived outdoors day and night; only man feared the evening dew. As advances were made in rearing methods, silkworms were raised first under the eaves, then outdoors, and finally were released into nearby trees. Sericulture appeared to be headed in the direction of natural farming when all of a sudden the industry fell upon hard times. The rapid development of synthetic fibers almost made natural silk obsolete. The price of silk plummeted, throwing sericulture farms out of business. Raising silkworms became regarded as something of a backwards industry. However, the growing material affluence of our times has nurtured extravagant tastes in people. Consumers rediscovered the virtues of natural silk absent in synthetic fibers, causing silk to be treated once again as something of a precious commodity. The price of silk cocoons skyrocketed and farmers regained an interest in silkworm cultivation. Yet by this time the hard-working farmer of old was gone, so innovative new sericulture techniques were adopted. These are purely scientific methods that go in a direction opposite to that of natural farming: industrial sericulture. Artificial feed is prepared from mulberry leaf powder, soybean powder, wheat powder, starch, fats, vitamins, and other ingredients. It also contains preservatives and is sterilized. Naturally, the silkworms are raised in a plant fully outfitted with heating and air conditioning equipment; lighting and ventilation are adjusted automatically. Feed is carried in, and droppings carried out, on a belt conveyor.

If disease should break out among the worms, the room can be hermetically sealed and disinfected with gas. With all feeding and cocoon collection operations fully automated, we have reached an age in which natural silk is something produced in factories. Although the starting material is still mulberry leaves, this will probably be replaced by a totally synthetic feed prepared from petrochemicals. Once an inexhaustible supply of cocoons can be produced in factories from a perfect diet, human labor will no longer be required. Will people then rejoice at how easily and effortlessly silk can be had in any amount? Sericulture has in this way shifted repeatedly from one side to another. From natural farming it moved to scientific farming, then appeared to move a step back in the direction of natural farming. However, once scientific farming begins to get under way, it does not regress or turn back but rushes madly onward along a path that takes it away from nature. The intertwining of natural farming and scientific farming can be depicted.

Narrowly defined natural farming, which includes organic farming, proceeds centripetally inward toward a state of "nothingness" (Mu) by the elimination of human labor; it compresses and freezes time and space. Modern scientific farming, on the other hand, seeks to appropriate time and space through complex and diverse means; it proceeds centrifugally outward toward "something-ness," expanding and developing as it goes. Both can be understood as existing in a relative relationship in the same dimension or plane. But although the two may appear identical at a given point, they move in opposite directions, the one headed for zero and the other for infinity. Thus, seen relatively and discriminatively, the two readily appear to be in opposition, yet intimately intertwined neither approaching nor moving away from one another, advancing together and complementarily through time. However, because natural farming condenses inward, seeking ultimately a return to the true world of nature that transcends the world of relativity, it is in irreconcilable conflict with scientific farming, which expands forever in the relative world. 2. The Four Principles of Natural Farming I have already shown how natural farming is clearly and undeniably superior to scientific farming, both in theory and in practice. And I have shown that scientific farming requires human labor and large expenditures, compounds chaos and confusion, and leads eventually to destruction. Yet man is a strange creature. He creates one troublesome condition after another and wears himself down observing each. But take all these artificial conditions away and he suddenly becomes very uneasy. Even though he may agree that the natural way of farming is legitimate, he seems to think that it takes extraordinary resolve to exercise the principle of "doing nothing." It is to allay this feeling of unease that I recount my own experiences. Today, my method of natural farming has approached the point of "doing nothing." I will admit that I have had my share of failures during the forty years that 1 have been at it. But because I was headed in basically the right direction, I now have yields that are at least equal to or better than those of crops grown scientifically in every respect. And most importantly: 1) my method succeeds at only a tiny fraction of the labor and costs of scientific farming, and my goal is to bring this down to zero; 2) at no point in the process of cultivation or in my crops is there any element that generates the slightest pollution, in addition to which my soil remains eternally fertile. There can be no mistaking these results, as I have achieved them now for a good many years. Moreover, I guarantee that anyone can farm this way. This method of "do-nothing" farming is based on four major principles: 1. No cultivation 2. No fertilizer 3. No weeding 4. No pesticides No Cultivation Plowing a field is hard work for the farmer and usually one of the most important activities in farming operations. In fact, to many people, being a farmer is synonymous with turning the soil with plow or hoe. If working the soil is unnecessary then, the image and reality of the farmer change drastically. Let us look at why plowing is thought to be essential and what effect it actually has. Plowing Ruins the Soil: Knowing that the roots of crops penetrate deep into the earth in search of air, water, and nutrients, people reason that making larger amounts of these ingredients available to the plants will speed crop growth. So they clear the field of weeds and turn the soil from time to time, believing that this loosens and aerates the soil, increases the amount of available nitrogen by encouraging nitrification, and introduces fertilizer into the soil where it can be absorbed by the crops. Of course, plowing under chemical fertilizers scattered over the surface of a field will probably increase fertilizer effectiveness. But this is true only for cleanly plowed and weeded fields on which fertilizer is applied. Grassed fields and no-fertilizer cultivation are a different matter altogether. We therefore have to examine the necessity of plowing from a different perspective. As for the argument that this helps increase available nitrogen through nitrification, this is analogous to wasting one's body for some temporary gain. Plowing is supposed to loosen the soil and improve the penetration of air, but does not this in fact have the opposite effect of compacting (he soil and decreasing air porosity? When a farmer plows his fields and turns the soil with a hoe, this appears to create air spaces in the soil and soften the dirt. But the effect is the same as kneading bread: by turning the soil, the farmer breaks it up into smaller and smaller particles which acquire an increasingly regular physical arrangement with smaller interstitial spaces. The result is a harder, denser soil. The only effective way to soften up the soil is to apply compost and work it into the ground by plowing. But this is just a short-lived measure. In fields that have been weeded clean and carefully plowed and re-plowed, the natural aggregation of the soil into larger particles is disturbed; soil particles become finer and finer, hardening the ground. Wet paddy fields are normally supposed to be tilled five, six, or even seven times during the growing season. The more zealous farmers have even competed with each other to increase the number of plowings. Everyone thought this softened the soil in the paddy and let more air into the soil. That is the way it looked to most people for a long time, until after World War II, when herbicides became available. Then farmers discovered that when they sprayed their fields with herbicides and reduced the frequency of plowing, their yields improved, This demonstrated that intertillage had been effective as a weeding process but had been worthless as a means for loosening the soil. To say that tilling the soil is worthless is not the same as claiming that it is unnecessary to loosen the soil and increase its porosity. No, in fact I would like to stress, more than anyone else, just how important an abundance of air and water are to the soil. It is in the nature of soil to swell and grow more porous with each passing year. This is absolutely essential for microorganisms to multiply in the earth, for the soil to grow more fertile, and for the roots of large trees to penetrate deep into the ground. Only I believe that, far from being the answer, working the soil with plow and hoe actually interferes with these processes. If man leaves the soil to itself, the forces of nature will enrich and loosen. Farmers usually plow the soil to a depth of about four to eight inches, whereas the roots of grasses and green manure crops work the soil down to twelve inches, fifteen inches, or more. When these roots reach down deep into the earth, air and water penetrate into the soil together with the roots. As these wither and die, many types of microorganisms proliferate. These organisms die and are replaced by others, increasing the amount of humus and softening the soil. Earthworms eventually appear where there is humus, and as the number of earthworm's increases, moles begin burrowing through the soil. The Soil Works Itself: The soil lives of its own accord and plows itself. It needs no help from man. Farmers often talk of "taming the soil" and of a field becoming "mature," but why is it that trees in mountain forests grow to such magnificent heights without the benefit of hoe or fertilizer, while the farmer's fields can grow only puny crops? Has the farmer ever given any careful thought to what plowing is? Has he not trained all his attention on a thin surface layer and neglected to consider what lies below that? Trees seem to grow almost haphazardly in the mountains and forests, but the cedar grows where it can thrive to its great size, mixed woods rise up where mixed woods must, and pine trees germinate and grow in places suited for pine trees. One does not see pines growing at the bottom of a valley or cedar seedlings taking root on mountain tops. One type of fern grows on infertile land and another in areas of deep soil. Plants that normally grow along the water's edge are not found on mountain tops, and terrestrial plants do not thrive in the water. Although apparently without intent or purpose, these plants know exactly where they can and should grow. Man talks of "the right crop for the right land," and does studies to determine which crops grow well where. Yet research has hardly touched upon such topics as the type of parent rock and soil structure suited to mandarin orange trees, or the physical, chemical, and biological soil structures in which persimmon trees grow well. People plant trees and sow seed without having the faintest idea of what the parent rock on their land is and without knowing anything about the structure of the soil. It is no wonder then that farmers worry about how their crops are going to turn out. In the mountain forests, however, concerns over the physical and chemical compositions of the topsoil and deeper strata are nonexistent; without the least help from man, nature creates the soil conditions sufficient to support dense stands of towering trees. In nature, the very grasses and trees, and the earthworms and moles in the ground, have acted the part of plow horse and oxen, completely rearranging and renewing the soil. What can be more desirable to the farmer than being able to work the fields without pulling a plow or swinging a hoe? Let the grasses plow the topsoil and the trees work the deeper layers. Everywhere I look, I am reminded of how much wiser it is to entrust soil improvement to the soil and plant growth to the inherent powers of plants. People transplant saplings without giving a thought as to what they are doing. They graft a scion to the stock of another species or clip the roots of a fruit sapling and transplant it. From this point on, the roots cease to grow straight and lose the ability to penetrate hard rock. During transplanting, even a slight entanglement of the tree's roots interferes with the normal growth of the first generation of roots and weakens the tree's ability to send roots deep into the soil. Applying chemical fertilizers encourages the tree to grow a shallow root structure that extends along the topsoil. Fertilizer application and weeding bring a halt to the normal aggregation and enrichment of topsoil. Clearing new land for agriculture by pulling up trees and bushes robs the deeper layers of the soil of a source of humus, halting the active proliferation of soil microbes. These very actions are what make plowing and turning the soil necessary in the first place. There is no need to plow or improve a soil because nature has been working at it with its own methods for thousands of years. Man has restrained the hand of nature and taken up the plow himself. But this is just man imitating nature- All he has really gained from this is a mastery at scientific exposition. No amount of research can teach man everything there is to know about the soil, and he will certainly never create soils more perfect than those of nature. Because nature itself is perfect. If anything, advances in scientific research teach man just how perfect and complete a handful of soil is, and how incomplete human knowledge. We can either choose to see the soil as imperfect and take hoe in hand, or trust the soil and leave the business of working it to nature. No Fertilizer Crops Depend on the Soil: When we look directly at how and why crops grow on the earth, we realize that they do so independently of human knowledge and action. This means that they have no need basically for such things as fertilizers and nutrients. Crops depend on the soil for growth. I have experimented with fruit trees and with rice and winter grain to determine whether these can be cultivated without fertilizers. Of course crops can be grown without fertilizer. Nor does this yield the poor harvests people generally believe. In fact, I have been able to show that by taking full advantage of the inherent powers of nature, one can obtain yields equal to those that can be had with heavy fertilization. But before getting into a discussion of why it is possible to farm without using fertilizers and whether the results are good or bad, I would like to look first at the road scientific farming has taken. Long ago, people saw crops growing in the wild and called this "growth." Applying discriminating knowledge, they proceeded from the notion of wild plant growth to plant cultivation. For example, scientists typically begin by analyzing rice and barley plants and identifying the various nutrients. They then speculate that these nutrients promote the growth of rice and barley. Next they apply the nutrients as fertilizer, and observing that the plants grow as expected, they conclude that the fertilizer is what makes the crops grow. The moment they compare crops grown with and without fertilizer and conclude that fertilizer application results in taller, better yielding plants, people cease to doubt the value of fertilizers. Are Fertilizers Realty Necessary?: The same is true when one delves into the reasons why fertilizers are thought to be essential to fruit trees. Pomologists normally begin with an analysis of the trunk, leaves, and fruit of the tree. From this they learn what the nitrogen, phosphorus, and potassium contents are and how much of these components are consumed per unit of annual growth or of fruit produced. Based on the results of such analyses, fertilization schedules for fruit trees in mature orchards will typically set the amount of nitrogen components at 90 pounds, say, and the amount of phosphates and potassium at 70 pounds each. Researchers will apply fertilizer to trees grown in test plots or earthen pots, and examining the growth of the tree and the amount and quality of fruit it bears, will claim to have demonstrated the indispensability of fertilizer. Learning that nitrogenous components are present in the leaves and branches of citrus trees and that these are absorbed from the ground by the roots, man hits upon the idea of administering fertilizer as a nutrient source. If this succeeds in supplying the nutrient needs of the leaves and branches, man immediately jumps to the conclusion that applying fertilizer to citrus trees is both necessary and effective. If one works from the assumption that fruit trees must "be grown," the absorption of fertilizer by the roots becomes the cause, and the full growth of the leaves and branches the effect. This leads quite naturally to the conclusion that applying fertilizer is necessary. However, if we take as our starting point the view that a tree grows of its own accord, the uptake of nutrients by the tree's roots is no longer a cause but, in the eyes of nature, just a small effect. One could say that the tree grew as a result of the absorption of nutrients by the roots, but one could also claim that the absorption of nutrients was caused by something else, which had the effect of making the tree grow. The buds on a tree are made for budding and so this is what they do; the roots, with their powers of elongation, spread and extend throughout the earth. A tree has a shape perfectly adapted to the natural environment. With this, it guards the providence of nature and obeys nature's laws, growing neither too fast nor too slow, but in total harmony with the great cycles of nature. The Countless Evils of Fertilizer: What happens when the farmer arrives in the middle of all this and spreads his fields and orchards with fertilizer? Dazzled and led astray by the rapid growth he hears of, he applies fertilizer to his trees without giving any thought to the influence this has on the natural order. As long as he cannot know what effects scattering a handful of fertilizer has on the natural world, man is not qualified to speak of the effectiveness of fertilizer application. Determining whether fertilizer does a tree or soil good or harm is not something that can be decided overnight. The more scientists learn, the more they realize just how awesome is the complexity and mystery of nature. They find this to be a world filled with boundless, inscrutable riddles. The amount of research material that lies hidden in a single gram of soil, a single particle, is mind-boggling. People call the soil mineral matter, but some one hundred million bacteria, yeasts, molds, diatoms, and other microbes live in just one gram of ordinary topsoil. Far from being dead and inanimate, the soil is teeming with life. These microorganisms do not exist without reason. Each lives for a purpose, struggling, cooperating, and carrying on the cycles of nature. Into this soil, man throws powerful chemical fertilizers. It would take years of research to determine how the fertilizer components combine and react with air, water, and many other substances in nonliving mineral matter, what changes they undergo, and what relationships should be maintained between these components and the various microorganisms in order to guard a harmonious balance. Very little, if any, research has been done yet on the relationship between fertilizers and soil microbes. In fact, most experiments totally ignore this. At agricultural research stations, scientists place soil in pots and run tests, but more likely as not, most of the soil microbes in these pots die off. Clearly, results obtained from tests conducted under fixed conditions and within a limited experimental framework cannot be applied to situations under natural conditions. Yet, just because a fertilizer slightly accelerates crop growth in such tests, it is praised lavishly and widely reported to be effective. Only the efficacy of the fertilizer is stressed; almost nothing is said about its adverse effects, which are innumerable. Here is just a sampling: 1. Fertilizers speed up the growth of crops, but this is only a temporary and local effect that does not offset the inevitable weakening of the crops. This is similar to the rapid acceleration of plant growth by hormones. 2. Plants weakened by fertilizers have a lowered resistance to diseases and pests, and are less able to overcome other obstacles to growth and development. 3. Fertilizer applied to soil usually is not as effective as in laboratory experiments. For example, it was recently learned that some thirty percent of the nitrogenous component of ammonium sulfate applied to paddy fields is denitrified by microorganisms in the soil and escapes into the atmosphere. That this came out after decades of use. is an unspeakable injury and injustice to countless farmers that cannot be laughed off as just an innocent mistake. Such nonsense will occur again and again. Recent reports say that phosphate fertilizers applied to fields only penetrate two inches into the soil surface. So it turns out that those mountains of phosphates that farmers religiously spread on their fields year after year were useless and were essentially being "dumped" on the topsoil. 4. Damage caused directly by fertilizers is also enormous. More than seventy percent of the "big three"—ammonium sulfate, super-phosphate, and potassium sulfate—is concentrated sulfuric acid which acidifies the soil, causing great harm to it, both directly and indirectly. Each year, some 1.8 million tons of sulfuric acid are dumped onto the farmlands of Japan in the form of fertilizer. This acidic fertilizer suppresses and kills soil microorganisms, disrupting and damaging the soil in a way that may one day spell disaster for Japanese agriculture. 5. One major problem with fertilizer use is the deficiency of trace components. Not only have we killed the soil by relying too heavily on chemical fertilizers, our production of crops from a small number of nutrients has led to a deficiency in many trace elements essential to the crops. Recently, this problem has risen to alarming proportions in fruit trees, and has also surfaced as one cause of low rice harvests. The effects and interactions of the various components of fertilizers in orchard soil are unspeakably complex. Nitrogen and phosphate uptake is poor in iodine-deficient soils. When the soil is acidic or turns alkaline through heavy applications of lime, deficiencies of zinc, manganese, boron, iodine, and other elements develop because these become less soluble in water. Too much potassium blocks iodine uptake and reduces the absorption of boron as well. The greater the amount of nitrogen, phosphate, and potassium administered to the soil, the higher the resulting deficiency of zinc and boron. On the other hand, higher levels of nitrogen and phosphate result in a lower manganese deficiency. Adding too much of one fertilizer renders another fertilizer ineffective. When there is a shortage of certain components, it does no good to add a generous amount of other components. When scientists get around to studying these relationships, they will realize just how complex the addition of fertilizers is. If we were prudent enough to apply fertilizers only when we were certain of the pros and cons, we could be sure of avoiding dangerous mistakes, but the benefits and dangers of fertilization are never likely to become perfectly clear. And the problems go on multiplying. Very limited research is currently underway on several trace components, but an endless number of such components remain to be discovered. This will spawn infinite new areas of study, such as mutual interactions, leaching in the soil, fixation, and relationships with microbes. Still, in spite of such intimidating complexity, if a fertilizer happens to be effective in one narrowly designed experiment, scientists report this as being remarkably effective without having the vaguest idea of its true merits and drawbacks. "Well yes," the farmer all too easily reasons. "Chemical fertilizers do cause some damage. But I've used fertilizers now for years and haven't had any big problems, so I suppose that I'm better off with them." The seeds of calamity have been sown. When we take note of the danger, it will be too late to do anything about it. Consider also the fact that farmers have always had to struggle to scrape together enough to buy fertilizer. Why, to give one simple example, fertilizers currently account for thirty to fifty percent of the costs of running an orchard. People claim that produce cannot be grown without fertilization, but is it really true that crops do not grow in the absence of fertilizer? Is the use of fertilizers economically advantageous? And have methods of farming with fertilizers made the lot of farmers easier? Why the Absence of No-Fertilizer Tests?: Strange as it may seem, scientists hardly ever run experiments on no-fertilizer cultivation. In Japan, only a handful of reports have been published over the last few years on the cultivation of fruit trees without fertilizer in small concrete enclosures and earthen pots. Some tests have been done on rice and other grains, but only as controls. Actually, the reason why no-fertilizer tests are not performed is all too clear. Scientists work from the basic premise that crops are to be grown with fertilizer. "Why experiment with such an idiotic and dangerous method of cultivation?" they say. Why indeed. The standard on which fertilizer experiments should be based is no-fertilizer tests, but three-element tests using nitrogen, phosphorus, and potassium are the standard actually used. Quoting the results of a very small number of insignificant experiments, scientists claim that a tree grows only about half as much without fertilizer as when various types of fertilizer are used, and the common belief is that yields are terrible—on the order of one-third that obtained with fertilizers. However, the conditions under which these nofertilizer experiments were conducted have little in common with true natural farming. When crops are planted in small earthenware pots or artificial enclosures, the soil in which they grow is dead soil. The growth of trees whose roots are boxed in by concrete is highly unnatural. It is unreasonable to claim that because plants grown without fertilizer in such an enclosure grow poorly, they cannot be grown without fertilizers. No-fertilizer natural farming essentially means the natural cultivation of crops without fertilizers in a soil and environment under totally natural conditions. By totally natural cultivation I mean no-fertilizer tests under "condition-less" conditions. However such experiments are out of the reach of scientists, and indeed impossible to perform. I am convinced that cultivation without fertilizers under natural circumstances is not only philosophically feasible, but is more beneficial than scientific, fertilizer-based agriculture, and preferable for the farmer. Yet, although cultivation without the use of chemical fertilizers is possible, crops cannot immediately be grown successfully without fertilizers on fields that are normally plowed and weeded. It is imperative that farmers think seriously about what nature is and provide a growing environment that approaches at least one step closer to nature. But to farm in nature, one must first make an effort to return to that natural state which preceded the development of the farming methods used by man. Take a Good Look at Nature: When trying to determine whether crops can be grown without fertilizers, one cannot tell anything by examining only the crops. One must begin by taking a good look at nature. The trees of the mountain forests grow under nearly natural conditions. Although they receive no fertilizer by the hand of man, they grow very well year after year. Reforested cedars in a favorable area generally grow about forty tons per quarter-acre over a period of twenty years. These trees thus produce some two tons of new growth each year without fertilizer. This includes only that part of the tree that can be used as lumber, so if we take into account also small branches, leaves, and roots, then annual production is probably closer to double, or about four tons. In the case of a fruit orchard, this would translate into two to four tons of fruit produced each year without fertilizers—about equal to standard production levels by fruit growers today. After a certain period of time, the trees in a timber stand are felled, and the entire surface portion of the tree—including the branches, leaves, and trunk—is carried away. So not only are fertilizers not used, this is slash-and-burn agriculture. How then, and from where, are the fertilizer components for this production volume supplied each year to the growing trees? Plants do not need to be raised; they grow of their own accord. The mountain forests are living proof that trees are not raised with fertilizer but grow by themselves. One might also point out that because the planted cedars are not virgin forest, they are not likely to be growing under the full powers of the natural soil and environment. The damage caused by repeated planting of the same species of tree, the felling and harvesting of the timber, and the burning of the mountainside take their toll. Anyone who sees black wattle planted in depleted soil on a mountainside and succeeded a number of years later with giant cedars many times their size will be amazed at the great productive powers of the soil. When black wattle is planted among cedar or cypress, these latter thrive with the help of the microbes present on the roots of the black wattle. If the forest is left to itself, the action of the wind and snow over the years weathers the rock, a layer of humus forms and deepens with the fall of leaves each year, microorganisms multiply in the soil— turning it a rich black, and the soil aggregates and softens, increasing water retention. There is no need for human intervention here. And the trees grow on and on. Nature is not dead. It lives and it grows. All that man has to do is direct these vast hidden forces to the growth of fruit trees. But rather than using this great power, people choose to destroy it. Weeding and plowing the fields each year depletes the fertility of the soil, creates a deficiency of trace components, diminishes the soil's vitality, hardens the topsoil, kills off microbes, and turns rich, living, organic material into a dead, inanimate, yellowish-white mineral matter the only function of which is to physically support the crops. Fertilizer Was Never Needed to Begin With: Let us consider the farmer as he clears a forest and plants fruit trees. He fells the trees in the forest and carries them off as logs, taking the branches and leaves as well. Then he digs deep into the earth, pulling up the roots of trees and grasses, which he burns. Next, he turns the soil over and over again to loosen it up. But in so doing, he destroys the physical structure of the soil. After pounding and kneading the soil again and again like bread dough, he drives out air and the humus so essential to microorganisms, reducing it to a yellow mineral matter barren of life. He then plants fruit saplings in the now lifeless soil, adds fertilizer, and attempts to grow fruit trees entirely through human forces. At agricultural research centers, fertilizer is added to potted soil devoid of life and nutrients. The effect is like sprinkling water on dry soil: the trees thrive on the fertilizer nutrients. Naturally, researchers report this as evidence of the remarkable effectiveness of the fertilizer. The farmer simulates the laboratory procedure by carefully clearing the land of all plant matter and killing the soil in the field, then applying fertilizer. He too notes the same startling results and is pleased with what he sees. The poor farmer has taken the long way around. Although I would not call fertilizers totally useless, the fact is that nature provides us with all the fertilizers we need. Crops grow very well without chemical fertilizers. Since ancient times, rock outcroppings on the earth have been battered by the elements, first into boulders and stones, then into sand and earth. As this gave rise to and nurtured microbes, grasses, and eventually great, towering trees, the land became buried under a mantle of rich soil. Even though it is unclear how, when, and from where the nutrients essential to plant growth are formed and accumulate, each year the topsoil becomes darker and richer. Compare this with the soil in the fields farmed by man, which grows poorer and more barren each year, in spite of the large amounts of fertilizer constantly poured onto it. The no-fertilizer principle does not say that fertilizers are worthless, but that there is no need to apply chemical fertilizers. Scientific technology for applying fertilizers is basically pointless for the same reason. Yet research on the preparation and use of organic composts, which are much closer to nature, appears at first glance to be of value. When compost such as straw, grasses and trees, or seaweed is applied directly to a field, it takes a while for this to decompose and trigger a fertilizer response in the crops. This is because microbes help themselves to the available nitrogen in the soil, creating a temporary nitrogen deficiency that initially starves the crops of needed nitrogen. In organic farming, therefore, these materials are fermented and used as prepared compost, giving a safe, effective fertilizer. All the trouble taken during preparation of the compost to speed up the rate of fertilizer response, such as frequent turning of the pile, methods for stimulating the growth of aerobic bacteria, the addition of water and nitrogenous fertilizers, lime, superphosphate, rice bran, manure, and so forth—all this trouble is taken just for a slight acceleration in response. Because the net effect of these efforts is to speed up decomposition by at most ten to twenty percent, this can hardly be called necessary, especially since there already was a method of applying straw that achieved outstanding results. The logic that rejects grassed fields, green manure, and the direct application and plowing under of human wastes and livestock manure changes with time and circumstances. Given the right conditions, these may be effective. But no fertilizer method is absolute. The surest way to solve the problem is to apply a method that adapts to the circumstances and follows nature. I firmly believe that, while compost itself is not without value, the composting of organic materials is fundamentally useless. No Weeding Nothing would be more welcome to the farmer than not having to weed his fields, for this is his greatest source of toil. Not having to weed or plow might sound like asking for too much, but if one stops to think about what repeatedly weeding and running a plow through a field actually means, it becomes clear that weeding is not as indispensable as we have been led to believe. Is There Such a Thing as a Weed?: Does no one question the common view that weeds are a nuisance and harmful to the raising of crops? The first step that those who distinguish between crops and weeds take is to decide whether to weed or not to weed! Like the many different microorganisms that struggle and cooperate in the soil, myriad grasses and trees live together on the soil surface. Is it right then to destroy this natural state, to pick out certain plants living in harmony among many plants and call these "crops," and to uproot all the others as "weeds"? In nature, plants live and thrive together. But man sees things differently. He sees coexistence as competition; he thinks of one plant as hindering the growth of another and believes that to raise a crop, he must remove other grasses and herbs. Had man looked squarely at nature and placed his trust in its powers, would he not have raised crops in harmony with other plants? Ever since he chose to differentiate crop plants from other plants, he has felt compelled to raise crops through his own efforts. When man decides to raise one crop, the attention and devotion he focuses on raising that crop gives birth to a complementary sense of repulsion and hate that excludes all else. The moment that the farmer started caring for and raising crops, he began to regard other herbs with disgust as weeds and has striven ever since to remove them. But because the growth of weeds is natural, there is no end to their variety or to the labors of those who work to remove them. If one believes that crops grow with the aid of fertilizers, then the surrounding weeds must be removed because they rob the crop plants of fertilizer. But in natural farming, where plants grow of their own accord without relying on fertilizers, the surrounding weeds do not pose any problem at all. Nothing is more natural than to see grass growing at the foot of a tree; no one would ever think of that grass as interfering with the growth of the tree. In nature, bushes and shrubs grow at the foot of large trees, grasses spread among the shrubs, and mosses flourish beneath the grasses. Instead of cut-throat competition for nutrients, this is a peaceful world of coexistence. Rather than seeing the grasses as stunting shrub growth and the shrubs as slowing the growth of trees, one should feel instead a sense of wonder and amazement at the ability of these plants to grow together in this way. Weeds Enrich the Soil: Instead of pulling weeds, people should give some thought to the significance of these plants. Having done so, they will agree that the farmer should let the weeds live and make use of their strength. Although I call this the "no-weeding" principle, it could also be known as the principle of "weed utility." Long ago, when the earth began to cool and the surface of the earth's crust weathered, forming soil, the first forms of life to appear were bacteria and lower forms of plant life such as algae. All plants arose for a reason, and all plants live and thrive today for a reason. None is useless; each makes its own contribution to the development and enrichment of the biosphere. Such fertile soil would not have formed on the earth's surface had there been no microorganisms in the earth and grasses on the surface. Grasses and other plants do not grow without a purpose. The deep penetration of grass roots into the earth loosens the soil. When the roots die, this adds to the humus, allowing soil microbes to proliferate and enrich the soil. Rainwater percolates through the soil and air is carried deep down, supporting earthworms, which eventually attract moles. Weeds and grasses are absolutely essential for a soil to remain organic and alive. Without grasses growing over the surface of the ground, rainwater would wash away part of the topsoil each year. Even in gently sloping areas, this would result in the loss of from several tons to perhaps well over a hundred tons of soil per year. In twenty to thirty years, the topsoil would wash entirely away, reducing soil fertility to essentially zero. It would make more sense then for farmers to stop pulling weeds and begin making use of their considerable powers. Of course, it is understandable when farmers say that weeds growing wild in rice and wheat fields or under fruit trees interfere with other work. Even in cases where cultivation with weeds appears to be possible and even beneficial in principle, monoculture is more convenient for the farmer. This is why, in practice, one must adopt a method that utilizes the strength of weeds but also takes into account the convenience of farming operations—a "weedless" method that allows the weeds to grow. A Cover of Grass Is Beneficial: This method includes sod and green manure cultivation. In my citrus orchard, I first attempted cultivation under a cover of grass, then switched to green manure cultivation. Now I use a ground cover of clover and vegetables with no weeding, tillage, or fertilizer. When weeds are a problem, then it is wiser to remove weeds with weeds than to pull weeds by hand. The many different grasses and herbs in a natural meadow appear to grow and die in total confusion, but upon closer examination, there are laws and there is order here. Grasses meant to sprout do so. Plants that flourish do so for a reason; and if they weaken and die, there is a cause. Plants of the same species do not all grow in the same place and way; given types flourish, then fade in an ongoing succession. The cycles of coexistence, competition, and mutual benefit repeat themselves. Certain weeds grow as individuals, others grow in bunches, and yet others form colonies. Some grow sparsely, some densely, and some in clumps. Each has a different ecology: some rise up over their neighbors and overpower them, some wrap themselves around others in symbiosis, some weaken other plants, and some die—while others thrive—as undergrowth. By studying and making use of the properties of weeds, one weed can be used to drive out a large number of other weeds. If the farmer were to grow grasses or green manure crops that take the place of undesirable weeds and are beneficial to him and his crops, then he would no longer have to weed. In addition, the green manure would enrich the soil and prevent its erosion. I have found that by "killing two birds wity one stone" in this way, growing fruit trees and tending an orchard can be made easier and more advantageous than normal methods. In fact, from my experience, there is no question that weeding in orchards is not only useless, it is positively harmful. What about in the case of crops such as rice or barley? I believe that the coexistence of surface plants is true to nature, and that the no-weeding principle applies also to rice and barley cultivation. But because the presence of weeds among the rice and barley interferes with harvesting, these weeds have to be replaced with some other herb. I practice a form of rice-barley succession cropping in which I seed barley together with clover over the standing heads of rice, and scatter rice seed and green manure while the barley is up. This more nearly approaches nature and eliminates weeding. My reason for trying such a method was not that I was tired of weeding or wanted to prove that cultivation is possible without weeding. 1 did this but of dedication to my goals of understanding the true form of rice and barley and of achieving more vigorous growth and higher yields by cultivating these grains in as natural a way as possible. What I found was that, like fruit trees, rice and barley too can be grown without weeding. I learned also that vegetables can be grown in a state that allows them to go wild, without fertilizer or weeding, and yet attain yields comparable to normal methods. No Pesticides Insect Pests Do Not Exist: The moment the problem of crop disease or insect damage arises, talk turns immediately to methods of control. But we should begin by examining whether crop disease or insect damage exist in the first place. A thousand plant diseases exist in nature, yet in truth there are none. It is the agricultural specialist who gets carried away with discussions on disease and pest damage. Although research is done on ways to reduce the number of country villages without doctors, no studies are ever run to find out how these villages have managed to get by without doctors. In the same way, when people spot signs of a plant disease or an insect pest, they immediately go about trying to get rid of it. The smart thing to do would be to stop treating insects as pests and find a way that eliminates the need for control measures altogether. I would like to take a look now at the question of new pesticides, which has escalated into a major pollution problem. The problem exists because, very simply, there are no non-polluting new pesticides. Most people seem to believe that the use of natural predators and pesticides of low toxicity will clear up the problem, but they are mistaken. Many feel reassured by the thought that the use of beneficial insect predators to control pests is a biological method of control without harmful repercussions, but to someone who understands the chain of being that links together the world of living organisms, there is no way of telling which organisms are beneficial predators and which are pests. By meddling with controls, all man accomplishes is destruction of the natural order. Although he may appear to be protecting the natural enemies and killing the pests, there is no way of knowing whether the pests will become beneficial and the predator's pests. Many insects that are harmless in a direct sense are harmful indirectly. And when things get even more complex, as when one beneficial insect feeds on a pest that kills another beneficial insect which feeds on another pest, it is futile to try and draw sharp distinctions between these and apply pesticides selectively. Pollution by New Pesticides: With the problem of pesticide pollution, many await the development of new pesticides that: 1. have no adverse effects on animal cells and act by inhibiting enzymes specific to given insects, microorganisms, pathogens, plants, or whatever; 2. are degradable under the action of sunlight and microorganisms, and are totally nonpolluting, leaving no residues. The antibiotics blasticidin S and kasugamycin were released onto the market as new pesticides that meet these conditions, and used widely as preventive measures against rice blast disease amid great clamor and publicity. Another recent area of investigation in which many are placing much hope is pesticides prepared from biological components already present in nature, such as amino acids, fatty acids, and nucleic acids. Such pesticides, it is generally surmised, are not likely to leave residues. One other new type of pesticide discovered recently and reported as possibly nonpolluting is a chemical that suppresses metamorphosis-regulating hormones in insects. Insects' secrete hormones that control the various stages of metamorphosis, from the egg to the larva, the pupa, and finally the adult. A substance extracted from the bay tree apparently inhibits secretion of these hormones. Because these substances work selectively on only certain types of insects, they are thought to have no effects on other animals and plants. But this is incorrect and shortsighted. Animal cells, plant cells, and microorganisms are basically all quite similar. When a pesticide that works on some insect or pathogen is said to be harmless to plants and animals, this is merely a word game that plays on a very minor difference in resistance lo that substance. A substance that is effective on insects and microorganisms also acts, to a greater or lesser degree, on plants and animals. A pesticidal or bactericidal effect is referred to as phytotoxicity in plants and pollution in animals and man. It is unreasonable to expect a substance to work only on specific insects and microbes. To claim that something does not cause pesticide damage or pollution is to make small distinctions based on minor differences in action. Moreover, there is no knowing when these minor differences will change or turn against us. Yet, in spite of this constant danger, people are satisfied if a substance poses no immediate threat of damage or pollution and do not bother to consider the greater repercussions of its effects. This attitude of ready acceptance complicates the problem and aggravates the dangers. The same is true as well of microorganisms employed as biological pesticides. Many different types of bacteria, viruses, and molds are sold and used in a variety of applications, but what effect are these having on the biosphere? One hears a lot lately about pheromones. These are chemicals produced by organisms in minute quantities that trigger very profound physiological changes or specific behavioral reactions in other individuals. They may be used, for example, to attract the males or females of a given insect pest. Even the use of chemo-sterilants together with such attractants and excitants is conceivable. Sterilization can be achieved by a number of methods, such as destruction of the reproductive function by irradiation with gamma rays, the use of chemo-sterilants, and interspecific mating. But no evidence exists lo support the claim that the effects of sterilization are limited to just the insect pest. If, for instance, one insect pest were entirely eliminated, there is no knowing what might arise in its place. No one has any idea what effects a given sterilant used on one type of insect will have on other insects, plants, animals, or man for that matter. An action as cruel as ruining and annihilating a family of organisms will surely invite retribution. The aerial spraying of mountain forests with herbicides, pesticides, and chemical fertilizers is considered a success if a given weed or insect pest is selectively killed, or the growth of trees improved. But this Js a grave error that can prove most dangerous. Natural conservationists have already recognized such practices as polluting. Spraying herbicides such as PCP does more than just kill weeds. This acts also as a bactericide and fungicide, killing both black spot on living plants and the-many putrefactive fungi and bacteria on fallen leaves. Lack of leaf decomposition seriously affects the habitats of earthworms and ground beetles, on top of which PCP also destroys microorganisms in the ground. Treating the soil with chloropicrin will temporarily alleviate bacterial soft rot in Chinese cabbage and the daikon radish, but the disease breaks out again two years later and gets completely out of hand. This germicide halts the soft rot, but at the same time it also kills other bacteria that moderate the severity of the disease, leaving the field open to the soft rot bacteria. Chloropicrin also works against fusarium fungi and sclerotium fungi that attack young seedlings, but one cannot overlook the fact that these fungi kill other important pathogens. Is it really possible to restore the balance of nature by spraying an array of bactericides and fungicides like this into a soil populated with such a large variety of microbes? Instead of trying to bring nature around to his own designs with pesticides, man would be much wiser to step out of the way and lei nature carry on its affairs without his interference. Man is also kidding himself if he thinks that he can clear up the problem of weeds with herbicides. He only makes things harder on himself because this leaves hardy weeds resistant to herbicides or results in the emergence of totally unmanageable new strains of weed. Somebody has come up with the bright idea of killing off herbicide-resistant weeds such as Kentucky bluegrass that are spreading from road embankments by importing an insect pest which attacks the weeds. When this insect begins to attack crops, a new pesticide will have to be developed, setting into motion another vicious cycle-To illustrate just how complex the interrelationships between insects, microorganisms, and plants are, let us take a look at the pine rot epidemic spreading throughout Japan. The Root Cause of Pine Rot: Contrary to the generally accepted view, I do not think that the primary cause of the red pine disease that has afflicted so many forested areas of Japan is the pinewood nematode. Recently a group of pesticide researchers at the Institute of Physical and Chemical Research pointed to a new type of aohen-kin ("blue change mold") as the real villain, but the situation is more complicated than this. I have made a number of observations that throw some light on the true cause. 1. On cutting down a healthy-looking pine in an infected forest, new pathogenic fungi can be isolated from pure cultures of some forty percent of the trunk tissue. The isolated fungi include molds such as kurohen-kin ("black change mold") and three types of aohenkin, all of them new, undocumented pathogens foreign to the area. 2. Nematode infestation can be observed under a microscope only after a pine is a quarter- or half-withered. Actually, the new pathogenic fungi arrived before the nematodes, and it is on them that the nematodes are feeding, not the tree. 3. The new pathogenic fungi are not strongly parasitic, attacking only weakened or physiologically abnormal trees. 4. Wilting and physiological abnormalities of the red pines are caused by decay and blackening of the roots, the onset of which has been observed- to coincide with the death of the matsutake mushroom, a symbiont that lives on the roots of red pines. 5. The direct cause of the death of matsutake mushrooms was the proliferation of kurosen-kin ("black bristle mold"), a contributing factor for which was the increasing acidity of the soil. That red pine disease is not caused by just one organism became clear to me from 1) the results of experiments I conducted on healthy trees in which I inoculated nematodes directly into pines and placed long-horned beetles on the trees under a netting, all without ill effect, and 2) the observation that even when all insect pests are kept off the tree, the roots continue to rot, causing the tree to die. Matsutake mushrooms die when small potted pine saplings are subjected to conditions of extreme dryness and high temperature, and perish when exposed to a temperature of 30OC for one hour in a hothouse. On the other hand, they do not die in alkaline soil by the shore with fresh water nearby, or on high ground at low temperature. On the assumption that red pine disease is triggered by acidification of the soil and dying of the matsutake mushroom, followed first by parasitic attack by kurohen-kin and other mold fungi, then by nematode infestation, I tried the following methods of control. 1. Application of lime to reduce soil acidification; in the garden, this can be done by spraying with water containing bleaching powder. 2. Spraying of soil germicides; in gardens, the use of hydrogen peroxide solution and alcohol chloropicrin disinfection is also okay. 3. Inoculation of matsutake spores grown in pure culture to promote root development. These are the bare bones of my method of fighting pine disease, but what most troubles me now is that, although we may feel confident of our ability to restore garden trees and cultivate matsutake artificially, we are powerless to rehabilitate an ecosystem that has been disturbed. It is no exaggeration to say that Japan is turning into a barren desert. The loss of the small autumn matsutake means more than just the perishing of a mushroom; it is a solemn warning that something is amiss in the world of soil microbes. The first telltale sign of a global change in weather patterns will probably appear in microorganisms. Nor would it be surprising if the first shock wave occurred in the soil where all types of microorganisms are concentrated, or even in mycorrhiza such as matsutake, which form a highly developed biological community with very organic interactions. Essentially, the inevitable happened where it was meant to happen. Red pine is a hardy plant capable of growing even in deserts and on sandy beaches. At the same time, it is an extremely sensitive species that grows under the protection of a very delicate fungus. Man's ability to control and prevent red pine disease may be a litmus test of his capacity to halt the global loss of vegetation.

6

How Should Nature Be Perceived?

———❦———

Seeing Nature as Wholistic The central truth of natural farming is that nothing need be done to grow crops. I have learned this because non-discriminating knowledge has enabled me to confirm that nature is complete and crops more than capable of growing by themselves. This is not the theoretical hypothesis of a scholar in his study or the wishful thinking of an idler with an aversion to work; it is based on a total, intuitive understanding of the reality about self and nature wrested from the depths of doubt and skepticism in a deeply earnest struggle over the meaning of life. This is the source of my insistence that nature not be analyzed. Examining the Parts Never Gives a Complete Picture: This principle is extremely important, but since it is somewhat abstract, I will illustrate with an example. A scientist who wishes to know Mt. Fuji will climb the mountain and examine the rocks and wildlife. After having conducted geological, biological, and meteorological research, he will conclude that, he now has a full picture of Fuji. But if we were to ask whether it is the scientist who has spent his life studying the details of the mountain who knows it best, the answer would have to be no. When one seeks total understanding and comprehensive judgment, analytic research is instead a hindrance. If a lifetime of study leads to the conclusion that Fuji consists mostly of rocks and trees, then it would have been better not to have climbed it in the first place. One can know Fuji by looking at it from afar. One must see it and yet not examine it, and in not examining it, know it. Yet the scientist will think: "Well, gazing at Mt. Fuji from a distance is useful for knowing it abstractly and conceptually, but is no help in learning something about the actual features of the mountain. Even if we concede that analytic research is of no use in knowing and understanding the truth about Fuji, learning something about the trees and rocks on the mountain is not totally meaningless. And moreover, isn't the only way to learn something to go and examine it directly?" To be sure, I can say that analyzing nature and appending to these observations one's conclusions is a meaningless exercise, but unless those who listen understand why this is worthless and unrelated to the truth, they will not be convinced. What more can I say if, when I mention that the artist Hokusai who captured faraway images of Fuji in his paintings understood it better than those who climbed it and found it an ugly mountain, I am told that this is just a subjective difference, a mere difference in viewpoint or opinion. The most common view is that one can best know the true nature of Fuji by both listening to the ecologist speak of his research on its fauna and flora and looking at the abstracted form of Fuji in Hokusai's paintings. But this is just like the hunter who chases two rabbits and catches none. Such a person neither climbs the mountain nor paints. Those who say Fuji is the same whether we look at it tying down or standing up, those who make use of discriminating knowledge, cannot grasp the truth of this mountain. Without the whole, the parts are lost, and without the parts, there is no whole. Both lie within the same plane. The moment he distinguishes between the trees and rocks that form a part of the mountain and the mountain as a whole, man falls into a confusion from which he cannot easily escape. A problem exists from the moment man draws a distinction between partial, focused research and total, all-encompassing conclusions. To know the real Fuji, one must took at the self in relation to Fuji rather than at the mountain itself. One must look at oneself and Fuji prior to the self-other dichotomy. When one's eyes are opened by forgetting the self and becoming one with Fuji, then one will know the true form of the mountain. Become One with Nature: Farming is an activity conducted by the hand of nature. We must look carefully at a rice plant and listen to what it tells us. Knowing what it says, we are able to observe the feelings of the rice as we grow it. However, to "look at" or "scrutinize" rice does not mean to view rice as the object, to observe or think about rice. One should essentially put oneself in the place of the rice. In so doing, the self looking upon the rice plant vanishes. This is what it means to "see and not examine and in not examining to know." Those who have not the slightest idea what I mean by this need only devote themselves to their rice plants. It is enough to be able to work with detachment, free of worldly concerns. Laying aside one's ego is the quickest path to unity with nature. Although what I am saying here may seem as intangible and difficult to understand as the words of a Zen priest, I am not borrowing philosophical and Buddhist terms to spout empty theories and principles. I am speaking from raw personal experience of things grounded solidly in reality. Nature should not be taken apart. The moment it is broken down, parts cease being parts and the whole is no longer a whole. When collected together, all the parts do not make a whole. "All" refers to the world of mathematical form and "whole" represents the world of living truth. Farming by the hand of nature is a world alive, not a world of form. The instant he begins to ponder over the factors of crop cultivation and growth and concerns himself with the means of production, man loses sight of the crop as a whole entity. To produce a crop, he must comprehend the true meaning of a plant growing on the earth's surface, and the goal of production must derive from a clear vision of unity with the crop. Natural farming is one way to remedy the presumptions and conceits of scientific thought, which claims to know nature and says man produces crops. Natural farming "checks whether nature is perfect or imperfect, whether it is a world of contradiction. The task then is to establish and prove whether pure natural farming free of all vestige of the human intellect is indeed powerless and inferior, and whether farming based on the inputs of technology and scientific knowledge is truly superior. For several decades now, I have devoted myself to examining whether natural farming can really compete with scientific farming. I have tried to gauge the strength of nature in rice and barley cultivation, and in the growing of fruit trees. Casting off human knowledge and action, relying only on the raw power of nature, I have investigated whether "do-nothing" natural farming can achieve results equal to or better than scientific farming. I have also compared both approaches using man's direct yardsticks of growth and yield. The more one studies and compares the two, whether from the limited perspective of growth and yields, or from a broader and higher perspective, the clearer and more undeniable becomes the supremacy of nature. However, my research on natural farming has done more than just point out the faults of scientific farming. It has given me a glimpse of the disasters that the frightening defects of modern practices are visiting on mankind. Imperfect Human Knowledge Fails Short of Natural Perfection: Understanding the degree to which human knowledge is imperfect and inadequate helps one to appreciate just how perfect nature is. Scientists of all ages have sensed with increasing clarity the frailty and insignificance of human knowledge as man's learning grew from his investigations of the natural world around him. No matter how unlimited his knowledge may appear, there are hurdles over which man cannot pass: the endless topics that await research, the infinitude of microscopic and submicroscopic universes that even the rapid specialization of science cannot keep pace with, the boundless and eternal reaches of outer space. We have no choice then but to frankly acknowledge the frailty and imperfection of human knowledge. Clearly, man can never escape from his imperfection. If human knowledge is unenlightened and imperfect, then the nature perceived and built up by this knowledge must in turn always be imperfect. The nature perceived by man, the nature to which he has appended human knowledge and action, the nature which serves as the world of phenomenon on which science acts, this nature being forever imperfect, then that which is opposed to nature— that which is unnatural, is even more imperfect. And paradoxically, the very incompleteness of the nature conceived and born of human knowledge and action—a nature that is but a pale shadow of true nature—is proof that the nature from which science derived its image of nature is whole and complete. The only direct means for confirming the perfection of nature is for each individual to come into immediate contact with the reality of nature and see for himself. People must experience this personally and choose to believe or not believe. I myself have found nature to be perfect and am trying here only to present the evidence. Natural farming begins with the assumption that nature is perfect. Natural farming starts out with the conviction that barley seeds which fall to the earth will send up sprouts without fail. If a barley sprout should emerge then later wilt in midgrowth, something unnatural has occurred and one reflects on the cause, which originates in human knowledge and action. One never blames nature, but begins by blaming oneself. One searches unrelentingly for a way to grow barley in the heart of nature. There is no good or evil in nature. Natural farming admits to the existence neither of insect pests nor of beneficial insects. If a pest outbreak occurs, damaging the barley, one reflects that this was probably triggered by some human mistake. Invariably, the cause lies in some action by man; perhaps the barley was seeded too densely or a beneficial fungus that attacks pests was killed, upsetting nature's balance. Thus, in natural farming, one always solves the problem by reflecting on the mistake and returning as close to nature as possible. Those practicing scientific farming, on the other hand, habitually blame insect infestation on the weather or some other aspect of nature, then apply pesticides to exterminate the marauding pest and spray fungicides to cure diseases. The road diverges here, turning back to nature for those who believe nature to be perfect, but leading on to the subjugation of nature for those who doubt its perfection. Do Not Look at Things Relatively In natural farming, one always avoids seeing things in relative terms; should one catch sight of relative phenomena, one immediately tries to trace these back to a single source, to reunite the two broken halves. To farm naturally, one must question and reject scientific thinking, all of which is founded on a relative view of things: notions of good and poor crop growth, fast and slow, life and death, health and disease, large and small yields, major and minor gains, profits and losses. Let me now describe what constitutes a viewpoint that does not fall prey to relativistic perceptions so that I may help correct the errors committed by a relative view of things. From a scientific perspective, things are large or small, dead or alive, increasing or decreasing. But this view is predicated on notions of time and space, and is really nothing more than a convenient assumption. In the natural world which transcends time and space, there is, properly speaking, no large or small, no life or death, no rise or fall. Nor was there ever the conflict and contradiction of opposing pairs: right and left, fast and slow, strong and weak. If we go beyond the confines of time and space, we see that the autumn wilting of a rice plant can be understood as life passing into the seed and continuing on into eternity. Only man frets over life and death, gain and loss. A method of farming founded on the view of birth as the beginning and death as the end cannot help but be short-sighted. In the narrow scientific view, growth appears to be either good or poor, and yields either large or small, but the amount of sunlight reaching the earth stays constant and the levels of oxygen and carbon dioxide remain balanced in the atmosphere. This being so, why do we nevertheless see differences in growth and yields? The fault is usually man's. Man destroys the immutability and stability of nature either by himself invoking the notions of large and small, many and few, or by altering form and substance. These things become self-evident when viewed from a deeper and broader perspective or from a perspective in accordance with nature. Man generally finds value only in the harvest of grains and fruit. But nature sees both cereal grains and weeds, and all the animals and microorganisms that inhabit the natural world, as the fruit of the earth. Notions of quantity and size usually exist within a limited frame of reference. From a broader or slightly more relaxed perspective, these cease to be problems at all. When looking at nature from the standpoint of natural farming, one does not worry over minor circumstances; there is no need for concern over form, substance, size, hardness, and other peripheral matters. Such concerns only cause us to lose sight of the real essence of nature and shut off the road back to nature. Take Perspective That Transcends Time and Space I have said that to travel the road leading to a natural way of farming, one must reject the use of discriminating knowledge and not take a relativistic view of the world. Such rejection may be thought of as a means for attaining a perspective transcending time and space. A world without discrimination, an absolute world that passes beyond the reaches of the relative world, is a world that transcends space and time. When captive to the notions of space and time, we are capable only of seeing things circumstantially. Scientific farming is a method of farming that originates within the confines of time and space, but Mahayana natural farming comes into being only in a world beyond time and space. Thus, in striving to realize a natural way of farming, one must focus one's efforts on overcoming time and space constraints in everything one does. Transcending time and space is both the starting point and the destination of natural farming. Scientific farming, concerned as it is with harvesting so much from a given field over such-and-such a period of time, is confined within the limits of time and space. But in natural farming one must go beyond space and time by making decisions and achieving results supported by a position of freedom and a long-term and general perspective. To give an example, when an insect alights on a rice plant, science immediately zeros in on the relationship between the rice plant and the insect. If the insect feeds on juices from the leaves of the plant and the plant dies, then the insect is viewed as a pest. The pest is researched: it is identified taxonomically, and its morphology and ecology studied carefully. This knowledge is eventually used to determine how to kill it. The first thing that the natural farmer does when he sees this crop and the insect is to see, yet not see, the rice; to see and yet not see the insect. He is not misled by circumstantial matters; he does not pursue the scientific method of inquiry by observing the rice and insect or investigating what the insect is. He does not ask why, when, and from where it came, or try to find out what it is doing in his field. What then does he do? He reaches beyond time and space by taking the stance that there are no crops or pests in nature to begin with. The concepts of "raising plants" and "harmful insects" are just words coined by man based on subjective criteria grounded in the self; viewed in terms of the natural order, they are meaningless. This insect is thus a pest and yet not a pest. Which is to say that its presence in no way interferes with growth of the rice plant for there is a way of farming in which both the rice plant and the insect can coexist in harmony. Natural farming seeks to develop methods of rice cultivation in which the existence of "pests" poses no problem. It begins by first stating the conclusion and clearing up local and temporal problems in a way that fits the conclusion. Even leafhoppers, pests from the scientific viewpoint, do not always harm rice. The time and circumstances also play a part. When I say that it is necessary to examine things from a broad, long-range perspective, I do not mean that one must conduct difficult and highly specialized research. The scientist studies rice damage by a particular insect, but it would suffice to observe cases where the insect does no damage to the rice. Such cases invariably exist. Instances of damage are quite naturally accompanied also by instances of no damage. There may be immense damage in one field and none in another. Invariably too, there are cases in which the insects will not even approach the rice. Natural farming examines cases in which little or no damage occurs and the reasons why, based on which it creates circumstances where nothing is done, yet insect damage is nonexistent. One type of leaf hopper that attacks rice plants early in the growing season is the green rice leafhopper, which lives among the weeds in the levees between rice fields from winter to early spring. To rid the fields of these leafhoppers, burning the levee weeds is preferable to direct application of a leafhopper poison. But an even better way is to change the variety of weeds growing on the levees. The white-backed leafhopper and the brown leafhopper tend to appear during long spells of hot, humid weather, but break out in especially large numbers in the summer or fall in flooded fields of stagnant water. When the field is drained and the surface exposed to breezes so that it dries, spiders and frogs emerge in number, helping reduce damage to a minimum. The farmer need not worry about damage by leafhoppers if he cultivates healthy fields of rice. Nature is always showing man, somewhere and sometime, situations in which pests are not pests and do not cause real damage. Instead of holing up in laboratories, people can learn directly in the open classrooms of nature. Natural farming takes its departure from a perspective transcending time and space, and returns to a point beyond time and space. Man must learn from nature the bridge that links these two points. The real meaning of taking a transcendent perspective, in plain, down-to-earth terms, is to help provide both insect pests and beneficial insects with a pleasant environment in which to live. Do Not Be Led Astray by Circumstance To look at things from a perspective that transcends time and place is to prevent oneself from becoming captive to circumstance. Even science constantly tries to avoid becoming too wrapped up in details and losing sight of the larger picture. However, this "larger picture" is not the true picture. There is another view that is broader and more allencompassing. In nature, a whole encloses the parts, and a yet larger whole encloses the whole enclosing the parts. By enlarging our field of view, what is thought of as a whole becomes, in fact, nothing more than one part of a larger whole. Yet another whole encloses this whole in a concentric series that continues on to infinity. Therefore, while it can be said that to act one must intuitively grasp the true "whole" and include therein all small particulars, this cannot actually be done. Let us take an example from the world of medicine. The physician studies the stomach and intestines, examines the ingredients of various foods, and investigates how these are absorbed as nutrients by the human body. The common perception is that, as research becomes increasingly focused and parallel advances are made in broad interdisciplinary studies, nutritional science becomes an authoritative field in its own right with wide application. But for all we know, nutritional science, which was introduced to Japan from Western Europe, may have first been modeled on German beer drinkers or French wine lovers. Nutritional principles that work for them do not necessarily apply to the people of Africa, for example. The same radishes will be absorbed very differently and will have an entirely different nutritive value for the irritable city dweller afflicted by smog and noise pollution who eats his without secreting digestive juices, as compared with the tropical African who munches on his after a meal of wild game. Progress in medicine has brought us a whole host of dietary therapies, such as lowcalorie diets for people who want to lose weight, light diets for people with stomach problems, low-salt diets for people with bad kidneys, and sugarless diets for people with pancreatic ailments. But what happens when a person has problems with two or three organs? If this food is out and that one forbidden, then the poor fellow, unable to eat anything, could end up as thin as a dried sardine. It is a mistake to believe that as advances are made in a broad range of highly specialized fields, the scope of applications grows. We should not forget that the more highly specialized the research, the further it strays from a broad overall perspective. In an age before the development of nutritional science, before we gave any thought about what was good or bad for us, alt we knew was that to stay healthy, one should eat in moderation. Which has broader application? Which is more effective? Modern nutritional science with its specialized research or traditional admonitions for moderation at mealtime? Modern nutritional science may appear to have broader application because it considers all cases. Yet it forbids first one thing then another, so people keep running into walls and struggling with a lot of new problems. Cruder but complete, the simple knowledge that one should cut with moderation applies to all people and thus it works better. This is so because knowledge that is less discriminating has wider application. Be Free of Cravings and Desires The aim of scientific farming is to chase after the objects of man's desire, but natural farming does not seek to satisfy or promote human cravings. Its mission is to provide the bread of human life. This is all it seeks, no more. It knows how much is enough. There is no need to become caught up in man's cravings and attempts to expand and fortify production. What has the campaign in Japan to produce good-tasting rice over the last several years achieved? How much happier does it make us when a farmer throws himself into improving varieties and raising production in response to the vagaries of the consumer for "tasty" rice and barley. Only the farmer suffers, because nature strongly resists all his efforts to upgrade crops for minor gains in taste and sweetness. Do urbanites know the torments that farmers go through—declines in production, reduced crop resistance to diseases and pests, to give but a couple examples—when consumers demand the slightest improvement in flavor? Nature sounds warnings and resists man's unnatural demands. Only, it says nothing. Man must make reparations for his own sins. But he cannot forget the sweetness he has tasted. Once the cravings of the palate assert themselves, there is no retreating. No matter how great the labors that farmers must shoulder as a result, these are of no concern to the consumer. Scientific farming exalts and follows the example of the farmer working diligently to service the endlessly growing demands of city dwellers, who expect, as a matter of course, fresh fruit and beautiful flowers in all seasons. The fruits of autumn picked in the fields and mountains were beautiful and sweet. The beauty of flowers in a meadow was a thing to behold. Natural farming tries to enter the bosom of nature, not break it down from without. It has no interest in conquering nature, but seeks instead to obey it. It serves not man's ambitions, but nature, reaping its fruit and wine. To the selfless, nature is always beautiful and sweet, always constant. Because all is fundamentally one. No Plan Is the Best Plan If nature is perfect, then man should have no need to do anything. But nature, to man, appears imperfect and riddled with contradiction. Left to themselves, crops become diseased, they are infested by insects, they lodge and wither. But upon taking a good look at these examples of imperfection, we realize that they occur when nature has been thwarted, when man has fiddled with nature. If nature is left in an unnatural state, this inevitably invites failure, leading not only to imperfection, but even catastrophe. When nature appears imperfect this is the result of something man has done to nature that has never been rectified. When left to its proper cycles and workings, nature does not fail. Nature may act,, or may compensate or offset one thing for another, but it always does so while maintaining order and moderation. The pine tree that grows on a mountain rises up straight and true, sending out branches in all directions in a regular annular pattern. In keeping with the rule of phyllotaxy, the branches remain equally spaced as they grow, so no matter how many years pass, branches never crisscross or overlap and die. The tree grows in just the right way to allow all the branches and leaves to receive equal amounts of sunlight. But when a pine is transplanted into a garden and pruned with clippers, the arrangement of branches undergoes a dramatic change, taking on the contorted "elegance" of a garden tree. This is because, once it has been pruned, the pine no longer sends out normal shoots and branches. Instead, branches grow irregularly, crisscrossing every which way, bending, twisting, and overlapping with each other. By merely nipping the buds at the tips of a few shoots, conical citrus trees that had until then grown straight fork into a three-leader arrangement or assume a wineglass shape. The same is true of all trees. Once man comes into the act, a tree loses its natural form. In a tree of unnatural habit, the branches are in disarray, growing either too close together or too far apart. Diseases arise and insects burrow and nest wherever there is poor ventilation or inadequate exposure to sunlight. And where two branches cross, a struggle for survival ensues; one will thrive, the other die. All it takes to destroy the conditions of nature and transform a tree that lived in peace and harmony into a battleground where the strong consume the weak is to nip a few young buds. Although disruption of the order and balance of nature may have begun as the unintentional consequence of impulsive human deeds, this has grown and escalated to the point where there is no turning back. Once tampered with, the garden pine can never revert back again to being a natural -tree. All it takes to disturb the natural habit of a fruit tree is to nip a single bud at the end of a young shoot. When nature has been tainted and left unnatural, what remains? It is here that begins the never-ending toil of man. Two crisscrossing branches compete with each other. To prevent this, man must meticulously prune the garden pine each year. Snipping off the tip of a branch causes several irregular branches to grow in its place. The tips of these new branches must then be cut the next year The following year, the even larger number of new branches create even greater confusion, increasing the amount of pruning that has to be done. The same holds true for the pruning of fruit trees. A fruit tree pruned once must be tended for its entire life. The tree is no longer able to space its branches properly and grow in the direction it chooses. It leaves the decision up to the farmer and just sends out branches wherever and however it pleases without the least regard for order or regularity. Now it is man's turn to think and cut the branches not needed. Nor can he overlook those places where the branches cross or grow too densely together. If he does, the tree will grow confused; branches at the center will rot and wither, and the tree will become susceptible to disease and insects and eventually die. Man, therefore, is compelled to act-because he earlier created the very conditions that now require his action. Because he has made nature unnatural, he must compensate for and correct the defects arising from this unnatural state. Similarly, man's deeds have made farming technology essential. Plowing, transplanting, tillage, weeding, and disease and pest control—all these practices are necessary today because man has tampered with and altered nature. The reason a farmer has to plow his rice field is that he plowed it the year before, then flooded and harrowed it, breaking the clods of earth into smaller and smaller particles, driving the air out and compacting the soil. Because he kneads the earth like bread dough, the field has to be plowed each year. Naturally, under such conditions, plowing the field raises productivity. Man also makes crop disease and pest control indispensable by growing unhealthy crops. Agricultural technology creates the causes that produce disease and pest damage, then becomes adept at treating these. Growing healthy crops should take precedence. Scientific farming attempts to correct and improve on what it perceives as the shortcomings of nature through human effort. In contrast, when a problem arises, natural farming relentlessly pursues the causes and strives to correct and restrain human action. The best plan, then, is true non-action; it is no plan at all.

7

Natural Farming for a New Age

At the Vanguard of Modern Farming To some, natural farming may appear as a return to a passive, primitive form of farming over the road of idleness and inaction. Yet because it occupies an immutable and unshakable position that transcends time and space, natural farming is always both the oldest and the newest form of farming. Today, it presses on at the very leading edge of modern agriculture. Although the truth remains fixed and immobile, the heart of man is ever fickle and changing; his thinking shifts with the passage of time, with circumstances, and so he is forced to alter his means. He, and science with him, orbits forever about the periphery without reaching in to the truth at the center. Scientific farming blindly traces spiraling cycles in the tracks of science. Today's new technology will become the dated technology of tomorrow, and tomorrow's reforms will become the stale news of a later day. What is on the right today will appear on the left tomorrow and on the right the day after. While this wheel spins round and round, it expands and diffuses outward. Even so, things were better when man circled about the periphery while gazing from afar upon the truth at the center. Man today tries to leap outside of nature and truth altogether. Balanced against this centrifugal force are the centripetal forces, represented by efforts to return to nature and to see the truth that have managed only barely to maintain a balance. But the moment this thread connected to the core breaks, man will fly away from truth like a whirling stone. The danger has now arrived at the doorstep of science. Scientific farming has no future. Natural Livestock Farming The Abuses of Modern Livestock Farming: The storms of agricultural reform are beginning to ravage the good name of agricultural modernization. Let us look at a trend that has emerged in all farming technologies. One new livestock technology that has been spreading like wildfire throughout Japan is the mass raising of chickens, pigs, cattle, and other livestock and fowl in large facilities. The animals are fed preserved foods compounded from a very small amount of natural feed and liberal amounts of additives such as drugs, vitamins, and nutrients, all ostensibly for protecting health. This eliminates the necessity of rushing about to attend to every need of the livestock. The animal is efficiently raised by placing it in a narrow enclosure or cage just big enough to accommodate it but hardly allowing it to move about. The goal is to produce as much as possible on a narrow piece of land. There appear to be no problems with this method. In addition to being efficient, the work is less physically demanding and production is better than ever. But high-volume livestock farming encounters the problems of market supply and distribution of the product familiar in factory production. Beset by wildly fluctuating prices, the livestock farmer becomes totally caught up with concerns over his margins and profits. The quality of these products is in every way inferior to beef and eggs from cattle and fowl allowed to roam freely outdoors and to multiply and grow without restraint. What's more, because these animals have been raised on roughage packed with antibiotics, preservatives, flavor enhancers, hormones, and residual pesticides, there is also the concern that toxins harmful to the human body have accumulated in the beef and eggs. We have arrived in an age where beef is no longer beef and eggs are no longer truly eggs. What we have instead is merely the conversion of complete feed preparations into animal products. Livestock farming is no longer a form of agriculture practiced in nature. Unfertilized battery chickens are just machines for hatching factory-made eggs, while hogs and cows are merely factory-produced meat and milk-fabricating machines. These products could not possibly be wholesome. The point is that, regardless of whether the product is good or bad, one person can raise tens and hundreds of thousands of head efficiently with mass production techniques. But it is capital, not men, that today raises these animals. This is no longer the farmer's domain, but that of commercial houses which raise livestock in large factory-like operations. Natural Grazing h the Ideal: Is natural livestock farming old and outdated in contrast? Under the precepts of natural farming, livestock farming takes the form of open grazing. Cattle, pigs, and chickens fattened while free to roam at will on the open land under the sun's rays are a precious, irreplaceable source of food for man. The problem lies elsewhere—in the prejudiced view that sees natural farming as inefficient. Is grazing, which allows one person to raise hundreds of head without doing anything, really inefficient? Is it not, rather, the most efficient form of production there is? This is not to say that raising livestock freely in open meadows and forests is without its problems. There are poisonous plants, diseases, and ticks. Some would even call free grazing unhygienic. But most such problems are the consequence of human action and can be resolved. The basic premise that animals are perfectly capable of being born and living in nature is unassailable, and so, although solutions may require some very determined observation, there is always a way. The key is to raise the right animal in the right environment while letting nature be. Even fields covered with a thick growth of wild roses and creepers that seem worthless for grazing can be used to raise goats and sheep, which love to feed on these intractable shrubs and vines and could clean up the undergrowth in the densest jungle. There is no need to worry that cows or other animals cannot be raised in uncultivated pastures. They can be raised in mixed woods or even in mountain forests planted with Japanese cypress or pine. Grasses and underbrush have to be cut the first seven or eight years after planting trees on a mountain, but the labor of cutting the brush can be eliminated very nicely by raising cows. The grazing cattle may slightly damage a few young saplings along a fixed path through the cypresses, but the planted saplings will remain almost entirely unaffected. This may seem hard to believe, but it is only natural when we recall that animals in nature do not indiscriminately ravage anything unrelated to what they eat. Obviously, a natural forest would be even more ideal than a reforested area. In allowing animals to graze in the fields and mountains, -some people may worry about the presence of poisonous plants, but animals have an innate ability to tell these apart from other plants. If no longer able to do so, there is most certainly a reason why. Bracken, for example, may be a poisonous herb under certain conditions, but it grows in clusters. If a cow eats too much and suffers, something is probably wrong with the cow. Livestock bred by artificial insemination and raised on artificial milk formulas are more likely to have poor viability. Animals improved indiscriminately often show unanticipated defects. Breeding programs are usually opposed to nature and often result in the creation of unnaturally deformed creatures that man deludes himself into thinking are superior. It would be unreasonable, of course, to take modern, genetically upgraded livestock, release them suddenly in a forest, and expect to see an immediate improvement in results. But if the possibilities are studied with patience, a path should open up. At the very least, after habituating the animals to open grazing in the forests over the course of two or three generations, natural selection will take over and those animals adapted to nature will survive. Ticks and mites do present a problem, but the conditions under which parasites such as these arise vary considerably. There may be a great number at the southern edge of a wood, but very few along the northern edge. Infestation is generally limited in cool, breezy areas, and is closely related to humidity and temperature. The problem can be prevented by providing the right environment. It should suffice to raise hardier cattle and give some consideration to the protection and raising of beneficial insects that help control the tick population. It will also be necessary to stop thinking in terms of raising just cattle. What happens, for example, when we let pigs, chickens, and rabbits graze together with the cows in an orchard? The pigs like to root up the ground looking for the insects and earthworms they are fond of in valleys and damp areas; they are like small tractors that dig up the soil. Just sow some clover and grain in the turned soil, and with the cow and pig droppings, you should get a fine growth of pasturage. Once this pasture grass begins to nourish, then you should be able to raise chickens, goats, and rabbits in the same way. Today's livestock raised in large numbers and reduced to just so much standardized machinery, no longer receives the strength and grace of nature. As the products of human endeavor achieved through the power of science alone, they differ fundamentally from nature—which creates something from nothing—because they are merely processed goods, the transformation of one thing into another. Livestock production under factorylike conditions is generally thought to be efficient, but this is a nearsighted assessment based on a limited spatial and temporal frame of reference. The pitiful sight of fowl, pigs, and cattle confined to cages and unable even to move bears witness to the loss of nature of these animals and points also to man's alienation to and loss of nature. Both the farm worker directly engaged in the raising of livestock and the city dweller who consumes these food products lose their health and humanity as they turn away from nature. Livestock Farming in the Search for Truth: Scientific farming is content to think of conditional truth as the truth, but natural farming makes every effort to discard all premises and conditions and seek out a truth without conditions. For instance, in order to study a particular animal feed, scientific farming will give various formulations to cows chained in a barn (representing a certain set of environmental conditions), and judge the mixture producing the best results to be superior to the others (inductive experimentation). From this, it draws various conclusions about cattle feed, which it believes to be the truth. Natural farming does not follow this type of reasoning and experimental approach. Because its goal is unconditional truth it begins by examining the cow from a standpoint that disregards environmental conditions, by asking how the cow lives in open nature. But it does not immediately analyze what the cow eats when and where. Rather, it takes a broader perspective and looks at how a cow is born and grows. By paying too much attention to what the cow feeds on, we lose a broader understanding of how it lives and what its needs are. More is required to sustain life than just food. Nor are problems of sustenance resolved by food alone. Many other factors relate to life: weather, climate, living environment, exercise, sleep, and more. Even on the subject of food, what a cow does not eat, dislikes, or has low nutritive value is generally thought worthless, but may actually be indispensable in certain cases. We must therefore find a way, within the broad associations between man, livestock, and nature, of rearing animals that leaves them free and unrestrained. The very notion of "raising" livestock should not even exist in natural farming. Nature is the one that raises and grows. Man follows nature; all he needs to know is with what and in what manner cattle live. When he designs and builds a barn or a chicken coop, a farmer should not rely on his human reasoning and feelings. Even if the scientist conducts independent studies on such factors as temperature and ventilation and runs experiments in which he raises calves or chicks under given conditions, it is only natural that his results will show that these should be raised under cool conditions in summer and warm conditions in winter. The conclusion (scientific truth) that an optimum temperature is needed to raise the calves or chicks is a natural consequence of the method used to raise these, and certainly is not an immutable truth. Although high and low temperatures exist in nature, the notions of hot and cold do not. Although cattle, horses, pigs, sheep, chickens, and ducks all know or cold. "With our temperate climate in Japan, there never was a need to worry about whether the summer heat or winter cold was good or bad for raising animals. Heat and cold exist, and yet do not exist, in nature. One will never be wrong in starting with the assumption that the temperature and humidity are everywhere and at all times just right. The size, height, frame, construction, windows, floor, and other features of animal enclosures have been improved on the basis of diverse theories, but we have to return to the starting point and try making a fundamental turnabout. Without hot and cold, the barn is no longer necessary. All that is needed, for the convenience of man, is the smallest of sheds: perhaps a milking shed for the cows and a tiny chicken shed in which hens can lay their eggs. As for the animals, they will scratch and forage freely for food night and day under the open sky, find themselves a place to roost, and grow up strong and healthy. Disease has become a frequent problem lately in animal husbandry and because it is often a major factor in determining whether a livestock operation will succeed or fail, farmers are racking their brains to find a solution. This problem too will never really be solved unless farmers make their starting point the raising of healthy animals that do not contract diseases. Some eighty percent of Japan consists of mountains and valleys. One could probably fence off the entrance to one of those depopulated mountain villages that have lost their inhabitants to the cities and thus create a large, open grazing range for animals. I would like to see someone try an experiment on this scale. All sorts of domestic animals could be placed inside the enclosure and left to themselves for a number of years, after which we could go in and see what had happened. To summarize, then, scientific experiments always take a single subject and apply a number of variable conditions to it while making some prior assumption about the results. Natural farming, however, pushes aside all conditions, and knocking away the precepts from which science operates, strives to find the laws and principles in force at the true source. Unchanging truths can be found only through experiments free of conditions, assumptions, and notions of time and space. Natural Farming—In Pursuit of Nature There is a fundamental difference between nature and the doctrine of laissez-faire or non-intervention. Laissez-faire is the abandoning of nature by man after he has altered it, such as leaving a pine tree untended after it has been transplanted in a garden and pruned, or suddenly letting a calf out to pasture in a mountain meadow after raising it on formula milk. Crops and domestic animals are no longer things of nature and so it is already close to impossible to attain true Mahayana natural farming. But at least we can try reaching for Hinayana natural farming, which approaches closest to nature. The ultimate goal of this way of natural farming is to know the true spirit and form of nature. To do this, we can start by closely examining and learning from a laissez-faire situation before us. By observing nature that has been abandoned by man, we can make out the true form of nature that lies behind it. Our goal then is to carefully examine abandoned nature and learn of the true nature revealed when the effects of man's earlier actions are removed. But this will not suffice to know nature in its true form. Even nature stripped of all human action and influence is still only nature as seen through man's relativity, a nature clothed in the subjective notions of man. To follow the path of natural farming, one must tear the robes of human action from nature and remove the innermost garments of subjectivity. One must beware also of arbitrarily settling upon causal relationships on the basis of subjective human notions, or of drawing suppositions on the problems of accident and necessity or the association between continuity and discontinuity. One must first follow closely on nature's heels, rejecting all assumptions, knowledge, and action—not thinking, not seeing, not doing. That nature is God. The Only Future for Man Will humanity go on advancing without end? The people of this world seem to think that, although reality is rife with contradiction, development will continue forever in a process of sublation while wandering between right and left, and thesis-antithesissynthesis. Yet the universe and all it contains does not advance along a linear or planar path. It expands and grows volumetrically outward and must, at the furthest limit, rupture, split, collapse, disappear. But at a point beyond this limit, what should have vanished reverses its course and reappears, now moving centripetally inward, contracting and condensing. What has form vaporizes at the limits of development to a void, and the void condenses into a form and reappears, in a never-ending cycle of contraction and expansion. I liken this pattern of development to the Wheel of Dharma or a cyclone because it is identical to a cyclone or tornado, which compresses the atmosphere into a vortex, expanding and growing as it rages furiously, then eventually disintegrates and vanishes. Human progress also moves mankind toward collapse. The question is how, and in what manner, shall this ruin come about? I have sketched below how I believe this will inevitably occur and what man must do. The first stage of this collapse will be the breakdown of human knowledge. Human knowledge is merely discriminating knowledge. Having no way of knowing that this knowledge is really unknowable, man founders ever deeper into confusion through the collection and advancement of unknowable and mistaken knowledge. Unable to extricate himself from schizophrenic development, he ultimately brings upon himself spiritual derangement and collapse. The second stage will be the destruction of life and matter. The earth, an organic synthesis of these two elements, is being broken down and divided up by man. This is gradually depriving the natural world on the earth's surface of its equilibrium. Destruction of the natural order and the natural ecosystem will rob matter and life of their proper functions. Nor will man be spared. Either he will lose his adaptability to the natural environment and meet with self-destruction or he will succumb to instant ruin under a slight pressure from without, like an inflated rubber balloon ruptured by a small needle. The third stage will be failure, when man loses sight of what he must do. The industrial activity that expands relentlessly with developments in the natural sciences is basically a campaign to promote energy consumption. Its target has not been so much to boost energy production as to senselessly waste energy. As long as man continues to take the stance that he is "developing" nature, the materials and resources of the earth will go on drying up. Burdened by growing self-contradictions, industrial activity will grind to a halt or undergo unyielding transformations that shall usher in drastic changes in political, economic, and social institutions. Self-contradiction is most evident in the decline in energy efficiency. In his fascination with ever greater sources of energy, man has moved from the heat of the fireplace to electrical generation with a water wheel to thermal power generation to nuclear power. But he closes his eyes to the fact that the efficiency of these sources (ratio of total energy input to total energy output) has worsened exponentially in the same order. Because he refuses to acknowledge this, internal contradiction continues to accumulate and will soon reach explosive levels. Some scientists believe that if nuclear energy dries up we should then turn to solar energy or wind power, which are non-polluting and do not engender contradictions. But these will only continue the decline in energy efficiency and, if anything, will accelerate the speed at which man heads toward destruction. Until man notices that scientific truth is not the same as absolute truth and turns his system of values on its head, he will continue to rush blindly onward toward selfdestruction. There will then be nothing for him to do except sustain an attitude that enables him to survive without doing anything. Man's only work then will consist of the barest of farming essential for sustaining life. But since agriculture does not exist as an independent entity of and for itself, the farming he will practice will not be an extension of modern agriculture. Farming with small machinery was more energy efficient than modern large-scale agriculture using large implements, while farming with animal power was even more efficient. And no form of agriculture has better energy efficiency than natural farming. Once this becomes clear, people will realize for themselves what they must do. Only natural farming lies in the future. Natural farming is the only future for man.

1. Starting a Natural Farm Once the decision has been made to start farming the natural way the very first problem that comes up is where and on what type of land to live. Although some may share the woodsman's preference for the isolation and solitude of a mountain forest, the best course generally is to set up a farm at the foot of a hill or mountain. Weather is often most pleasant when the site is slightly elevated. Abundant firewood, vegetables, and other necessities are to be had here, providing all the materials required for food, clothing, and shelter. Having a stream nearby helps make crops easy to grow. This type of location thus provides all the conditions essential for setting up an easy and comfortable life. Of course, with effort, crops can be made to grow on any type of land, but nothing compares with richly endowed land. The ideal location is one where enormous trees tower above the earth, the soil is deep and a rich black or brown in color, and the water is clear. Scenic beauty perfects the site. A good environment in an attractive setting provides the physical and spiritual elements necessary for living a pleasant life. The natural farm must be able to supply all the materials and resources essential for food, clothing, and shelter. In addition to fields for growing crops, a complete natural farm should include also a bordering wood. Keep a Natural Protected Wood The woods surrounding a natural farm should be treated as a natural preserve for the farm and used as a direct or indirect source of organic fertilizer. The basic strategy for achieving long-term, totally fertilizer-free cultivation on a natural farm is to create deep, fertile soil. There are several ways of doing this. Here are some examples. 1. Direct burial of coarse organic matter deep in the ground. 2. Gradual soil improvement by planting grasses and trees that send roots deep into the soil. 3. Enrichment of the farm by carrying nutrients built up in the humus of the upland woods or forest downhill with rainwater or by other means. Whatever the means employed, the natural farmer must secure a nearby supply of humus that can serve as a source of soil fertility. When there is no uphill wood available for use as a preserve, one can always develop a new wood or bamboo grove for this purpose. Although the main function of a preserve is to serve as a deeply verdant natural wood, one should also plant companion trees that enrich the soil, timber trees, trees that supply food for birds and animals, and trees that provide a habitat for the natural enemies of insect pests. Growing a Wood Preserve: Being generally infertile and dry, hill and mountain tops are highly susceptible to denudation. The first thing to do is plant a vine such as kudzu to prevent the soil from washing away. Next, sow the seeds of a low conifer

such as moss cypress to create a mountain cover of evergreens. Grasses such as cogon, ferns such as bracken, and low bushes such as lespedeza, eurya, and moss cypress grow thickly at first, but this vegetation gradually gives way to urajiro (a fern), kudzu, and a mix of trees which further enriches the soil. Evergreens such as Japanese cypress and the camphor tree should be planted on hillsides, and together with these, deciduous trees such as Chinese hackberry, zelkova, paulownia, cherry, maple, and eucalyptus. Plant the fertile land at the foot of hills and in valleys with oak and evergreens such as cryptomeria and live oak, interplanting these with walnut and ginkgo. A bamboo grove may serve equally well as the reserve. It takes a bamboo shoot only one year to grow to full size, so the amount of vegetative growth is greater than for ordinary trees. Bamboo is therefore valuable as a source of coarse organic material that can be buried in the ground for soil improvement. Not only can the shoots of certain species of bamboo be sold as a vegetable, when dried the wood is light and easy to carry. Bamboo is hollow and so has a large void ratio, in addition to which it decomposes slowly. These properties help it to retain air and water in the soil when it is buried. Clearly then, this plant may be used to great advantage in the improvement of soil structure. Shetterbelts: Shelterbelts and windbreak trees are valuable not only for preventing wind damage, but also for maintaining soil fertility and for environmental improvement. Fast-growing trees that are commonly planted for this purpose include cedar, cypress, acacia, and the camphor tree. Other species that grow somewhat more slowly but are also used quite often include camellia, the umbrella tree, wax myrtle, and Chinese anise. In some places, evergreen oaks, holly, and other trees are also used. Setting Up an Orchard One may establish an orchard and plant nursery stock using essentially the same methods as when planting forest trees. Vegetation on the hillside is cut in lateral strips, and the large trunks, branches, and leaves of the felled trees are arranged or buried in trenches running along hill contours, covered with earth, and allowed to decompose naturally. None of the vegetation cut down in the orchard should be carried away. In modern orchards, using bulldozers to clear land has become the rule rather than the exception, but a natural farm should be developed without clearing the land. When land is cleared with a bulldozer, irregular surface features on a slope are flattened and smoothed. Wide farm roads are built to permit farm mechanization. However, mechanization really only facilitates certain farm operations such as fertilizer and pesticide application. Since picking ripened fruit is the only major operation in natural farming, there is no need to go out of one's way to clear steep slope. Another factor that improves the enterprising orchardist's chances of success is that a natural orchard can be established without a heavy initial outlay of capital or incurring large debts. Starting a Garden People usually think of a garden as a plot of land devoted to the production of vegetables and field crops. However, using the open space in an orchard to raise an undergrowth of special-purpose crops and vegetables is the very picture of nature. Nothing stops the farmer from having his orchard double as a vegetable and grain patch. Clearly, of course, the system of cultivation and the nature of the garden or orchard will differ significantly depending on whether the principal aim is to grow fruit trees or vegetable crops. Land to be used for growing fruit trees and intercropped with grains or vegetables is prepared in essentially the same way as an orchard. The land does not need to be cleared and leveled, but should be carefully readied by, for example, burying coarse organic material in the ground. When starting an orchard, the main goals initially should be prevention of weed emergence and maturation of the soil. These can be accomplished by growing buckwheat during the first summer, and sowing rapeseed and Indian mustard that same winter. The following summer, one may plant adzuki bean and mung bean, and in the winter, hairy vetch and other hardy leguminous plants that grow well without fertilizers. The only problem with these is that they tend to inundate the young fruit tree saplings. As the garden, matures, it will support any type of crop. The Non-Integrated Garden: Gardens are normally created on hillsides and welldrained fields at the foot of larger mountains. Most of the crops grown in these gardens are annuals and the period of cultivation is generally short, in most cases lasting from several months to about a half-year. Most vegetables rise to a height of no more than three feet or so and are shallowrooting. The short growing period allows this cycle to be repeated several times a year, subjecting the surface of the soil to considerable exposure to the sun. A dry-farmed field, then, is prone to erosion and soil depletion by rainfall, susceptible to drought, and has low resistance to the cold. Soil movement being the greatest concern when establishing a garden, the garden should be built in terrace fashion with the Surface of the field on each terrace level. The first task in setting up a garden is to build a series of lateral embankments or stone walls running across the slope of the hill. Knowledge of the soil and the ability to build earthen embankments that do not crumble or to skillfully lay stones dug up from the field can be a determining factor in the success of a garden. Whether the individual terraces in a terraced garden are level or slightly graded makes a large difference in crop returns and the efficiency of farming work. As I mentioned earlier, the most basic method for improving soil is to bury coarse organic matter in deep trenches. Another good method is to pile soil up to create high ridges. This can be done using the soil brought up while digging contour trenches with a shovel. The dirt should be piled around coarse organic material. Better aeration allows soil in a pile of this sort to mature more quickly than soil in a trench. Such methods soon activate the latent fertility of even depleted, granular soil, rapidly preparing it for fertilizer-free cultivation. Creating a Rice Paddy Today, a rice field can easily be prepared by clearing the land with large machinery, removing rocks and stones, and leveling the surface of the field. Yet, although well-suited to increasing the size of single paddy fields and promoting mechanized rice production, such a process is not without its drawbacks: 1) Because it is crude, it leaves a thickness of topsoil that varies with the depth of the bedrock, resulting in uneven areas of crop growth. 2) The load that heavy machinery places on the soil results in excessive settling, causing ground water to stagnate. This situation can induce root rotting and at least partial suppression of initial crop growth on the new field. 3) Levees and walkways are all made of concrete, upsetting and destroying the community of soil microbes. The danger here is of gradually turning the soil into a dead mineral matter. Traditional Paddy Preparation: Most people might expect open, level ground to be the most sensible place on which to set up rice paddies. But rather than settling on the flat and fertile banks of large rivers, Japanese farmers of old chose to live in mountain valleys where there was far less cause to fear violent flooding and strong winds. They set up small fields in the valleys or built terraced rice fields on the hillsides. To these farmers, the work of digging channels for drawing water from the valley steams, of constructing rice fields, and of building rock walls and terraced fields was not as hard as the people of today imagine. They did not think of it as hardship. By spreading the field with the cuttings from ridge grasses, bordering weeds, and young foliage from trees, rice could easily be grown each year without using fertilizers. A tiny field of maybe a hundred square yards supplied the food needs for one individual indefinitely. The spiritual peace and security, the simple joy of creating a rice paddy were greater than can be imagined. From these activities, our farming ancestors gained pleasure and satisfaction of a sort that cannot be had through mechanized farming. I can recall occasionally happening upon small paddy fields deep in the mountains far from populated areas and my surprise at how well someone had managed to set up a field in such a location. To the modern economist, this would appear as utter wretchedness, but I found the field a wonderful masterpiece reminiscent of the past—built alone by someone living happily in the seclusion and quiet solitude of the wilds with nature as his sole companion. In truth, this place, with its artfully built conduit snaking in the shade of valley trees for drawing water, the rockwork that displays a thorough knowledge of the soil and terrain, and the beauty of the moss on the stones, was in reality a splendid garden built with great care by an anonymous farmer close to nature who drew fully on the resources about him. As the agrarian scenes of yesterday are rapidly swept off by the tide of modernization, we might do well to consider whether we can afford to lose the aesthetic spirit of our farming forbears, who saw the rice paddy as the arbor of their souls and gazed upon a thousand moons reflected in a thousand paddies. But of one thing I am certain: fields and rice paddies imbued with this spirit will reappear again somewhere, someday. These are not just the fond recollections of bygone days by a misty-eyed old fogey. The general method of establishing a rice paddy I have described here accords with reality as it exists on uncultivated open plains and meadows. Crop Rotation Modern farming has brought about destruction of the soil and a loss in soil fertility because it breaks crops up into many different use categories and grows each in isolation, often single-cropping continuously over extensive areas. On the complete natural farm, fruit trees, vegetables, grains, and other crops must all be planted and grown in an organic and mutually favorable arrangement. More specifically, a reliable crop rotation scheme must be established in order to be able to make essentially permanent use of the land while maintaining soil fertility. Fruit trees must not be dissociated from the trees of a bordering wood or the weed undergrowth. Indeed, it is only by having intimate associations with these that they are able to show normal, healthy growth. As for vegetables, when left to themselves in a field, they appear at first glance to grow without order, but these develop into splendid plants while nature solves the problems of continuous cropping, space, disease and pest damage, and the recovery of soil fertility. Ever since primitive man began slash-and-burn agriculture, the question of what crops to plant when has been the greatest problem faced by farmers everywhere. Yet a clearly decisive system of crop rotation has yet to be established. In the West, systems of rotation based on pasturage have been established for some time, but because these were designed for the benefit of ranchers and their animals rather than for the land itself, they have brought about a decline in soil fertility that calls for immediate improvement. In Japan as well, although farmers do grow a wide variety of different crops using an excellent system of crop rotation, a basic crop rotation scheme worthy of more widespread use has yet to be developed. One reason for this is the staggering number of possible crop combinations, and the essentially infinite number of elements that must be considered in stabilizing and increasing yields. To bring all these together into a single system of crop rotation would be an exceedingly difficult undertaking. The diagrams on the following pages are intended to serve as aids to an understanding of crop rotation. Rice/Barley Cropping: Japanese farmers have long practiced the continuous rotation of rice with barley. This has enabled them to reap the same harvest year after year indefinitely, something which they have always regarded as perfectly natural. Yet this type of rotational cropping is an extraordinary method of farming that has taken hold nowhere else in the world. The reason rice and barley can be grown in continuous succession each year is that the rice is grown in paddy fields, the soil fertility of which has been built up by a superior method of irrigation. To tell the truth, I am proud of the outstanding cultivation methods developed by Japanese farmers and would like to see these introduced abroad. Still, some very simple yet significant improvements could be made. For example, about seventy percent of the nitrogenous components absorbed by rice and barley are supplied directly by the soil, while about thirty percent are furnished artificially by fertilization. If all the straw and chaff from the threshed grain were returned to the fields, farmers would only have to apply at most fifteen percent of the nitrogenous components required by the plants. Reports have begun appearing recently in scientific journals on the possibilities of developing cultivars of rice not requiring fertilization. These propose the creation of strains of rice capable of fixing nitrogen by incorporating the root nodule genes of soybeans into rice genes, One has to admit, though, that nature has achieved a smarter method of non-fertilizer cultivation. True, because my method of rice-barley cropping under a cover of green manure is, in a sense, just a mimicry of nature, it is incomplete in itself. But there remains much that man can and should try before he resorts to genetic engineering, a technology with the frightening potential to utterly destroy nature. Upland Rice: Wheat and rice are each the staple foods of about half the world's population, but if the cultivation of upland rice were to spread and this grain became easy to harvest in high yield, a large jump would occur in the number of rice-eating peoples. Growing upland rice could even possibly become one effective way of coping with the worldwide scarcity of food. Generally speaking, upland rice is an unstable crop often subject to drought. Yields are lower than for rice grown in paddy fields, and continuous cropping gradually depletes soil fertility, resulting in a steady decline in yields. A workable solution appears to be rotational cropping in combination with various green manure crops and vegetables, as this raises the ability of the soil to retain water and gradually builds up soil fertility. Minor Grains: This group includes members of the grass family such as millet and corn, as well as buckwheat, Job's tears, and other grains. Compared with rice, barley, and wheat, these grains generally receive short shrift because of their "inferior" taste and a lack of research on methods for their use, but they deserve more attention for their very great value as prototypic health foods essential for maintaining the physical well-being of human beings. The same is true also for vegetables and other plants in general. The wilder and more primitive the food, the greater its medicinal value. With changes in popular taste, the cultivation of these minor grains as food for man has rapidly receded to the point where even seed preservation has become difficult. Yet, above and beyond their importance as a food for humans and animals, they have also played a vital role as coarse organic matter essential for soil preservation. When singlecropped or grown continuously, these grains deplete the soil, but if rotated with green manure crops and root vegetables, they improve and enrich the soil. This is why I believe the minor grains should be repopularized. Vegetables: People tend to think of vegetables as frail crops that are difficult to grow, but with the exception of several types that have been genetically over-improved, such as the cucumber and tomato, these are surprisingly hardy crops that can thrive even under extensive cultivation. Cruciferous winter vegetables, for example, when sown just before the emergence of weeds, grow vigorously, overwhelming the weeds. These also send down roots deep into the soil, and so are highly effective in soil improvement. That leguminous green manure suppresses summer weeds and enriches the soil hardly needs repeating. Clearly these too should play an important part in a crop rotation. Judicious combinations of vegetables in a sensible mixed cropping scheme can be grown in fair yield, free of disease and pest damage, without resorting to pesticides. I have found also, through personal experience, that most vegetables, when cultivated in a semi-wild state that could be considered a natural rotation, can be grown almost entirely without fertilizers. Fruit Trees and Crop Rotation: Because fruit trees are continuously cultivated perennials, they are subject to the difficulties associated with continuous cropping. The purpose of having a protected wood and a ground cover of weeds is to resolve such problems naturally and extend the life of the fruit trees. These trees exist, together with the companion-planted manure trees and the weed undergrowth, in a three-dimensional rotational cropping relationship. When vegetables are grown beneath fruit trees, the number of insect pests tends to be low. Some diseases and pests are common both to fruit trees and vegetables, and some are not. These in turn have a host of different natural enemies that emerge at various times of the year. As long as a balance is maintained between the fruit trees, the vegetables, the insect pests, and their natural predators, real damage from disease and insect attack can be prevented. For the same reason, the planting of manure trees and windbreak trees, and the combination planting of evergreens and deciduous trees may also be helpful in diminishing damage. In most cases, serious disease and pest damage in fruit trees, such as by long-horned beetles and scale insects, is triggered by diminished tree vigor due to depleted soil fertility, a confused tree shape, poor ventilation, inadequate light penetration, or a combination of all of these factors. Because they help sustain soil fertility, a ground cover of green manure crops and the combination planting of manure trees may thus be regarded as basic defensive measures against disease and pest damage. Using natural farming methods to cultivate fruit trees creates a truly three-dimensional orchard. More than just a place for growing fruit, the orchard becomes an organically integrated community that includes fowl, livestock, and man as well. If a natural orchard is managed and run as a single microcosm, there is no reason why one should not be able to live self-sufficiently. By looking with equal detachment at insects, which man categorizes as beneficial or harmful, people will see that this is a world of coexistence and mutual benefit, and will come to understand that farming methods which call for heavy inputs of fertilizer and energy can only succeed in robbing the land of its natural fertility. Nature is sufficient in and of itself; there never was a need for human effort and knowledge. By returning to a "do-nothing" nature, all problems are resolved.

www.ingramcontent.com/pod-product-compliance
Lightning Source LLC
Chambersburg PA
CBHW070839160726
48004CB00001B/436